Master Print maker and Fronterizo artist Francisco Enrique Delgado grew up in Juarez, Chihuahua - Mexico. His paintings have graced countless book covers, national art exhibitions, prestigious art galleries, private collections, and community institutions. He has a Bachelor in Fine Arts from the University of Texas at El Paso and a Masters in Fine Arts from the Yale School of Art.

Francisco believes in making visible the struggles of immigrant people throughout the United States. Due to his Mex-Tex Border upbringing, Francisco's imagery reflects and targets political views and events that negatively affect the Fronterizo way of life. His visual representations are commitments to art-making that demonstrates the survival of under-represented communities. By doing so, such as in the case of the Pelo Bueno book artwork, Mr. Delgado transcends perimeters and unites communities in a language of universal truth.

PELO BUENO

BUENO

A Day in the Life of a Nuyorican Poet

Pelo Bueno is dedicated to:
my family, my mother, my sister, my father, grandmother, grandfather, aunts, uncles, and cousins who put up with me on the holidays when I play my guitar and recite my poetry.

PELO BUENO

A Day in the Life of a Nuyorican Poet

BY BONAFIDE ROJAS

Edited with a Foreword by Louis Reyes Rivera
Introduction by Shaggy Flores

Dark Souls Press
Arlington, VA

Printed in Canada
Hignell Book Printing
488 Burnell Street
Winnipeg - Manitoba, Canada
R3G 2B4
www.hignell.mb.ca/home.html

First Edition

For information about permission to reproduce selections from this
book, contact Dark Souls Press.

www.nuyoricanpoetry.com

Front Cover Artwork by Francisco Delgado
Edited by Louis Reyes Rivera
Photographs by Johnette Ellis, S.R.B., Shaggy Flores
Design and Layout by Dark Souls Graphics

ISBN   0-9706307-1-9

Dark Souls Press
P.O. BOX 41522
Arlington, VA 22204

Para mi gente who were there from the Alpha to the Omega:

Perry, Angel, Wilfredo, TCK, Reals, Vaz, Dage, Sege, Kels, Chris Geeron, Bzar, Smirk, Sabe, 175th, Chris, Red, Will, Rob, Wes, Paul, Al, Timmy, Louie, Marcus, Landi, Jay, Rash, Bethany, Dark Souls Collective, Kevin Coval, Dennis Kim, Saulo Colon, Joey, Mission, Gina, Jessie, Dara, Shaggy Flores, Willie Perdomo, Tony Medina, Mike Ladd, GRFX, Jessica Care Moore, Shariff Simmons, Saul Williams, Sunday Tea Party, Nuyorican Poets Cafe, Bar 13, Guy, Roger, Lynne, Marty, Ed, Bassey, Oscar, Fish, Sabrina, Eric, Seve, Louder Arts, Beau Sia, Krystal Ashe, Anacron, 2 Tongues, Mango Tribe, Dan Sullivan, SeeMore Perspective, Itch 13, Anna West, YCA, Bob Boone, Jenn, Koz, Alanna, Lamon, Booker, Derrig, Woods, Nikki P., Tara Betts, Joel Chmara, The Guild Complex, Rhea, Toni, Ellen, Karimi, Emily, Jose, Mara, Ceaser, Moises, Phil, Ron, Dre, Ozzy, The Lozanos, Rudy, Pepe, David, Lupe, Leticia, Jose Hernandez, Alba Hernandez, T&W, Louis Reyes Rivera, Pedro Pietri, Sandra Maria Esteves, Juan Flores, Raul Salinas, The Baraka's Amiri, Amina, Ras, Jorge Matos, Vincent Ramirez, Yerba Buena, Universes, Villalobos, Giles Li, Marina, Michelle Mai, Dennis D., Yolanda, Youth Speaks, James Kass, Bamuthi, Paul S. Flores, Mateo, Melinda, The Suicide Kings, Charles Ellick, Emily K., Patricia Smith, Eitan Kadosh, Rives, Bullhorn Collective, Buddy Wakefield, Jeff Kass, Rebecca, Caleb, PSI Inc., Oscar Sanchez, Milton Rosado, Dolores Huerta, LCLAA, AFL-CIO, Nueva Esperanza, William and Mary College, Texas A&M - SCOLA, Old Dominion University, Brian & LSA, Virgina Commonwealth College, Nassau County Community College, Bowling Green University, SMART, Gear Up, George Meany Labor Center, Julie Mendez, Labor Heritage Foundation, Colgate University, Queen Sheba, Oyaxclusive, Open Square, Voices for the Voiceless, La Causa, Campos H.S., Centro PR, MACLA, Howard University, ASPIRA of NY, MUEVETE, Dean Bell, Mark Schwartz, Eduardo Suarez, Jim Crow Museum of Racist Memorabilia, NILC, Jimi Hendrix, The Beatles, Nirvana, Rage Against the Machine, Tribe called Quest, Public Enemy, BDP, Arsonists, Bobbito, Typical Cats, Pacifics, Juggaknots, System of a Down, At The Drive-In, Mars Volta, Red Hot Chili Peppers, Radiohead, and all those that provided inspiration to the soundtrack of my life.

Hair Care Products - Handle with Care

Hair Care Products - Handle with Care

A Bonafide Context
On Behalf of Our Continuum

What informs the poetry of Steven Bonafide Rojas?

If we pay attention only to his Now, our range of measurement would go no further than to place his work within the context of immediate trends. Hip Hop. Rap. Spoken Word. Graffiti Art. But these phenomena did not come upon the earth self-created. There's the historic implication here that cannot be missed or dismissed. A continuum to which he and those immediate trends belong. And it's right there in his work, in those numerous shout-out allusions to which he gives due props —Pedro Albizu Campos, Jimi Hendrix, Lolita Lebron, Ernesto Che Guevara, Federico Garcia Lorca, Jean Michel Basquiat, e.e. cummings, Julia de Burgos, Pablo Neruda, Amiri Baraka, Sonia Sanchez, Assata Shakur, Malcolm X, Langston Hughes, Ernesto Cardenal, Jose Marti, Pedro Pietri, Bob Dylan, Muddy Waters, B.B. King, John Lee Hooker, Camus, Coltrane, Garcia Marquez, Ginsberg, Picasso, Shakespeare & Chango. What to do with that? With them? With his sense of roots?

How do we account for a Puerto Rican Rojas born and bred in the Bronx? Is his family a community of migrants or transplants? That is to ask, with what degree of self-initiated choice does a Puerto Rican family move from Guanica to New York City? *Migrant* speaks more to personal choices made. *Transplant* speaks more to a set of existing conditions imposed from without. The difference between the two speaks to the degrees to which conditions dictate choices made. Finally, what exactly is a Puerto Rican, or even an American, for that matter?

There's a history here we should not ignore, a context that helps to explain the thought process working to shape a line, a poem, another book contributing to a specific collective stream of thought and contemplation. Consider...

...Back in 1493, Christopher Columbus brought to the island of Quisqueya Bohio Ayiti (now Haiti and the Dominican Republic) 17 ships, 1500 passengers, sufficient numbers of cotton and sugar cane seedlets, cows, pigs and hound dogs. This second European voyage into the Caribbean marks the beginning of chattel slavery in the Americas and the creation of the hemisphere's first cop (note that *cop* has long been a constant metaphor in the urban/urbane poetry of African and Latino Americans).

The goods they brought tell us something about intent — pigs and cows for raising meat; cotton and sugar cane for mass production and export. The assortment of immigrants is also informative — colonists, administrators, commercialists, mercenaries and a solid number of European slaves and servants brought directly from Spain —Moors (Muslim and otherwise), Jews, Christians too tolerant to be counted on (i.e., the true targets of a Spanish Inquisition), and a caste of working poor, including captured West Africans shipped and sold by the Portuguese who, since 1450, had been competing in Europe against a theretofore exclusive Muslim slave trade that itself dates back to 800 AD.

But most telling are the hound dogs themselves. They speak of the underlying intent to enslave the Amerindians who had first greeted them, to import Africans along with an initial European caste into the Caribbean as supplemental to an indigenous labor force, and to safeguard against runaways (a la Nina Simone's lyrics: "hound dogs on my trail..."). Thus, the first cop in the Americas was a bounty hunter. Thus, the first Rainbow Coalition, as we understand the category, comprising those who refused and resisted against the imposition, giving rise to Maroon settlements, guerilla war and buccaneering.

Six European nations (Spain, Portugal, England, France, The Netherlands, Denmark) separately invaded, conquered and established competing settler colonies dependent on slavery throughout the Americas. In the same breath of moment, tens of thousands of those who were the objects of slavery did what they could to fight back. In short, what began in 1493 became hallmark to the hemispheric social struggle against slavery and colonialism, those two underlying pillars of American history hemispherically written in blood and guts and voice.

Witness the North American Revolution of 1776, declaring war against colonizers along with the claim that commercial and business interests can govern themselves without the benefit of monarch or priest. Tax cheats and smugglers constitutionalizing their greed and thievery. Those remarkable documents, the Declaration of Independence and the Bill of Rights, while professing on behalf of natural citizenship, the inalienable rights of men, did not mean to include other than white Anglo-Saxon Protestant businessmen (WASPs), thus keeping chattel slavery relatively intact in the new United States for another 90 years.

Witness the Haitian Revolution (1791-1804), initiated by Maroons, enjoined by slaves and eventually a freedmen caste, taking on and defeating the three major powers of that day (France, Spain, England), and establishing the first republic in the Americas to immediately outlaw slavery.

Beginning with Mexico in 1809, and by 1824, one by one, each of the Spanish colonies in Central and South America had followed the Haitian model. No more chattel. No more colonies. Between 1834 and 1840, each of the British colonies had been forced by the slaves themselves (particularly behind large scale Maroon wars in Guiana and slave insurrections in Jamaica) to abolish slavery in order to keep the empire intact. The French followed suit in 1848, the Dutch in 1861, and finally the United States in 1865, but only after a bloody civil war.

Between 1884 and 1888, the last bastions of this chattel system had been finally eliminated in Puerto Rico, Cuba and Brazil. Within this revolutionary epoch (1791-1888), the British, having understood the inevitable, began to supplant its Atlantic Slave Trade by gradually increasing the numbers of indentured servants shipped from Central and Eastern Asia and sold (or contracted) into Caribbean basin countries straight through into the 1920s.

Meanwhile, by 1898, the U.S. government, under the control of its own major corporations, had established both an internal and external frame for neoslavery. Inside the United States, this neoslavery manifested in juridical manipulation of existing laws, vis a vis, fugitive slave laws built into the Constitution, the Dred Scott Decision, Plessy vs. Ferguson, etc. Thus, racial discrimination and segregation, extralegal imprisonment, sharecropping systems, urban and industrial exploitation of the working poor, disfranchisement, public lynchings, police brutality and semi-sanctioned race riots became the modes of operation for an imposed second class noncitizenship status upon the children of the formerly enslaved.

Outside of the U.S., it took the form of international corporate expansion —usurping the Cuban and Filipino revolutions (1895-98), invading and recolonizing a virtually sovereign Puerto Rico, overthrowing, intervening or collaborating against practically every other sovereign nation in the hemisphere, including Mexico, Haiti, the Dominican Republic, Cuba, Guatemala, Nicaragua, Colombia, Panama,

Chile, Peru, Ecuador, Brazil, etc. Here, then, the underlying practical application of a U.S. foreign policy dictated by a corporate destiny manifesting itself. With the exception of *Castro's Cuba*, the rest of the Americas has since remained dominated by U.S.-based corporations in true neocolonialist fashion, as the continued colonization of Puerto Rico remains the clearest symbol of a northern agenda (witness Vieques).

While this form of neoslavery dominates both the political and economic spheres of human activity, it has never been able to totally dominate the cultural sphere.

From the viewpoint and interests of the children of the enslaved, if there were such a phenomenon as an American BC and AD, it would be the year 1888.

Before 1888, the concern of the dispossessed was freedom. Emancipation. Liberation. Sovereignty. It began with the first runaways who established independent strongholds as Maroons or as Buccaneers, raiding both plantation and sea lane. It soared with small and large scaled slave insurrections, as well as with individual acts of sabotage, burning crops just harvested or poisoning food just served. This ultimate and basic concern embedded itself within and without the dominant culture, as Africans and Amerindians moved to preserve something of themselves, their culture, into the culture and even into the belief systems of those who had enslaved them. As with Santeria and Voodoo, the hemisphere's oppressed communities insistently worked their Mojo in the cultural sphere of self-expression to thus affectuate the social arena, creating and preserving their own mythology as essential to human struggle. Freedom Songs, Praise and Work Songs, folklore, coded Blues and coded Spirituals, Mambo, Samba, Plena, Bomba. And so not only the veil of a double consciousness (a la W.E.B. Du Bois' *The Souls of Black Folk*), but as well two separate and concurrent streams of valued expression, of thought and action, of those spiritual guideposts that affirm a political perspective and give credence to the potential for economic development. One such stream, what is called the mainstream, has ever been corporately controlled, i.e., the dictatorship of white over Black. The other, what is often viewed as a parallel sidestream, thrives and thrusts forward on its own terms despite the limitations often imposed from without, i.e., that which is "indigenous" to the given community.

Thus, out of a movement against slavery and colonialism comes the substance of a Culture of Resistance, along with and practically beside a corresponding Literature of Resistance, establishing its own canon and from the viewpoint of the oppressed. And this literature is much older than now. For when European nations began to export printing presses into their colonies (circa 1730, among the British; since 1750 in the Spanish and French Caribbean), it was not just colonists or sympathizers who published their tracts, poems, novels, treatises, speeches, newspapers and journals. Freed folk and slaves also learned to read, write, propagate against tyranny and slavery, stoking the fires of outcry and outburst —rallies, conferences, conventions, conspiracies, uprisings, liberation movements, marronage, guerilla war —all of it taking place throughout the Americas in a massive, rippling effort to "tear this building down," a la the spiritual, *If I Had'a My Way*.

Once chattel slavery ends, the coded agenda changes from *freedom* to *access*, full and equal access to all things human.

Since 1888, straight through to tomorrow, the children and grandchildren of the formerly enslaved now begin to expand upon their own social construct. That Culture of Resistance is now a Culture of Affirmation, a Renaissance of self-definition, with each subsequent generation adding onto the particular cosmology. And this must be understood from the viewpoint that it is hemispheric, even while the two most impactive groupings are quantitatively those who speak Spanish and English, and that the mixtures and blends we all comprise in whatever degrees have triple roots, stemming as they do from Amerindian, African and European cultures.

In this process of self-definition, we have had to learn that our perspective is as much inherited as it is what each generation itself shapes as further contribution. We inherit not only a capacity to do and a compulsion to defend ourselves through each of our own particular root, but as well the social conditions that come with class/caste imposition as well as the political baggage rooted in the contentions between those six European powers that had imposed themselves upon the rest of us (English, Spanish, French, etal) —not only a desire to reclaim and aspire, but the pitfalls of provincial thought that harness our prejudices as well (note the 'tudes and contentions between Haitians and Dominicans, between British West Indians and Spanish Antilleans, between North and South Americans—each of which is an outgrowth of white supremacy). Right alongside this psychotic baggage, however, there arise Race Men, Negritudists, Hispanophiles, communalists, cultural and revolutionary nationalists —all of them giving form to Art and Artist, and more precisely to the Cultural Workers among us —those who consciously help to forge a people's self-esteem (or, as poet Zizwe Ngafua would have it, "the one[s] who [see] what most have forgotten how to see...") in every arena of self-expression —literature, art, music, dance, philosophy, fashion.

Thus, the basis for a renaissance manifesting since 1888, in which the descendants of a Chatteled America learn to define themselves. Thus, Ragtime, the Blues, Gospel, Swing, Merengue, Calypso, Ska, Salsa, Reggae, Funk & Fusion, Free Jazz, BeBop, CuBop, Doo Wop, Hip Hop, the birth of the Cool —the spirit of intellect giving voice to its own voice. Thus, unionism, socialism, communism, anarchism, Garveyism, Pan-Africanism, nationalism, and a straight up claim to sovereignty standing against continued imperialism. Thus, a National Negro Renaissance in the U.S., Negrismo in Cuba, diepalismo and criollismo in P.R. and D.R., Reggae and Dub out of Jamaica and into the rest of the Caribbean, the Black Arts and Nuyorican Poetry movements out of New York City and unto the planet.

Hip Hop, Rap and Spoken Word are but the more current manifestations of that engagement, in the same manner that Funk has one root in the Blues and the other in BeBop, like Break Dancing, rooted in an African martial art, is capoeira revisited, as the thrust towards affirmation provides its own outlet even among the untutored.

Now read Bonafide. A new Nuyorican Poet who, unlike many of the Spoken Worders grasping for the glitter and the glimmer of a momentary spotlight, has actually read and studied something that goes beyond the existential present. (Research the names he drops, and you'll see it, paying homage to the continuum of social struggle.)

Philosophically, he embraces his Amerindian and African self, the principle of concentric circles (No Beginning, No End), one American whole, exploring and exposing us to his own reflection upon a condition older than his years. With this first book, clearly he demonstrates the potential of our current crop of cultural workers in search of substance. Here, the personal is as political as the risks many dare not take, as each poem presented here testifies to the dual function of art —exploring the individual particular and cajoling the community from which it hails to weigh the possibility that we can indeed reshape our own respective destinies.

Louis Reyes Rivera
Shamal Books
June 2, 2003

Pelo Bueno y Pelo Malo
Nuyorican Poetics in the New Millennium

Since the advent of the Atlantic slave trade, the notion of Good Hair versus Bad Hair has haunted members of the African Diaspora. Hair, as a political tool, has come to epitomize the struggle between self-acceptance and the concept that all things European or flaxen haired are inherently beautiful. Through the use of multimedia outlets, advertisements reinforce the superiority of straight hair. Even when African Diaspora models are used in these advertisements, their hair texture tends to be abnormally similar to their European counterparts. The history and the political ramifications, combined with the continuous messages relating to the supremacy of flaxen hair, all converge in the minds of members of the African Diaspora, producing a drive to achieve the European standard of beauty. In this quest, naturally short curly hair (what many have been conditioned to see as 'kinky') is subjected to pulling, wrapping, hot combs, and various chemical processes. Fortunes, like that of Madame CJ Walker, have been made at the expense of self-dignity.

Hair straightening is not the only manifestation of the elusive desire to assimilate. Other industries, such as skin lightening creams, have also emerged to feed this hunger. The difference between other industries and the hair care industry is that while skin lightening creams have become marginalized, the quest for straight hair has embedded itself so deeply into the subconsciousness of the Diaspora that it is now unacceptable for a woman with kinky hair *not* to straighten it. Wearing one's hair in a natural style can be the cause of a range of reactions from being passed over in corporate promotions to eliciting frowns from fellow Diasporics.

Fast-forward to the early 1990's. It is the annual Puerto Rican Day parade in New York City. In a sea of oscillating bodies there is one figure that stands out from the crowd, a young poet with a large Afro blowing in the wind. He and his Afro stood together in defiance of the hair police and the notion of Pelo Malo/Pelo Bueno. On that day, in that crowd, I met Steven "Bonafide" Rojas, a poet whose full head of hair stood as a proclamation that embodied the spirit of the Nuyorican and Black Arts movements.

Immediately, *Pelo Bueno* is Bonafide's attempt to create a space for a dialogue and for an introspective journey into the concept of "Pelo Bueno" (Good Hair) and "Pelo Malo" (Bad Hair). In flipping the script, as we say in the Barrio, the reader is challenged to view kinks or naps as elements of beauty and to question the presumption that one's own natural features are somehow undesirable and subject to elimination. With the Afro or Natural, we find the elegance of a people who have overcome slavery and its ramifications. Gone are the minstrel shows of the 19th and 20th centuries. Through this book, the poet replaces those images with resurrected memories of the Young Lords, Brown Berets, and Black Panthers proclaiming loudly that they are "Black and Proud!" and that among them are an Afro-Taino People!

But *Pelo Bueno* does not stop short as a simple social commentary on issues of identity, racism, and psychology within the Diaspora. It also serves as an in-depth look into the life and times of a New Generation Nuyorican poet. A poet who is among those now at the forefront of a literary movement that began in the 1930's, solidified itself in the 1970's, and transformed into the current Spoken Word Revolution seen on cable television. Through Bonafide's poetry you see the Puerto Rican experience told by an emerging artist who believes, as Nuyorican scholar Louis Reyes Rivera would point out, that there are poets... compelled to serve as cultural workers on behalf of the disinherited.

Bonafide Rojas uses language and contemporary music to challenge the norms and status quo. Through his use of language, the rhythms of Hip-Hop/Rock & Roll speak with a Bronx Boogie attitude that reflects his Nuyorican roots. A child of the Puerto Rican Diaspora transplanted to the streets of Nueva Yol, Mr. Rojas uses his words as blades, cutting through the absurdity and deceit that often plague our judgment.

In the tradition of Julia De Burgos, Clemente Soto Velez, Pedro Pietri, Victor Hernandez Cruz, Tato Laviera, and the many others who have pushed a Puerto Rican literary canon, Bonafide Rojas holds his place within this esteemed group. Through poems like *Creed of a Graffiti Writer*, *Invisible Ones*, and *25 Years In*, we see the maturity of a writer spitting in the wind, his Nommo creating poems that resurrect ancestors and endorse empowerment. While many in the Nuyorican canon would be content with poems that speak to their personal experiences, Mr. Rojas chooses to personalize issues of oppression and cultural preservation. His dialectic focuses on several themes—the immigrant experience in America, tales of wasted talent in an Andy Warhol Era, and visions of war in faraway lands speak with clarity and power.

Not only does the poetry in *Pelo Bueno* call for academia and the literary establishment to take a deeper look at the Nuyorican experience, it also serves to teach and encourage future generations to preserve their literature. With one of the highest illiteracy and drop out rates in the country, the Black and Puerto Rican communities benefit when one of its own bards delivers a tool for reaching forgotten youth.

Through his live readings across the country, email requests for samples of his poetry, national Slam competitions, and youth poetry workshops, Bonafide has made it clear where his poetry lives and breathes. *Pelo Bueno*, in all of its beauty, resides in the heart of transglobal Barrios where the poor congregate to tell their stories of survival and perseverance. This book is a convergence of Bochinches and Encuentros, mixed with rhythmic verse and B-Boy, Beat-Box body bravado. Break-Dancing in the pages of *Pelo Bueno* are tales of neither here nor there and the futility that faces a people pushed to the borderlands of Imperialism. Bonafide navigates carefully, his pen moves, we watch, read, listen, and hope that tomorrow the next poem will remind scholars that an artist committed to his craft can never be denied.

Pa'lante, Bonafide! Pa'lante!

Jaime "Shaggy" Flores
Nuyorican Poeta
May 26, 2003

Braids and Twists

the 4th son of Hip-Hop
overshadowed by Technic table microphones
and Puma's gray suede complexion tone

The Creed of a Graffiti Writer

One man's fight for love

Let me say at the risk of appearing ridiculous that a true
revolutionary is guided by a strong sense of love - Che Guevara

When I cradle the title poet
I will be the voice of them
I will speak of the survivors of Hiroshima
the cancer babies of Vieques
echoes of Diallo
the whispers of a mother scorned
an F# of a trumpet horn
the voice of a shadow between bars
workers in California grapevines, Uvas no
priests of Latin American Liberation Theology

I will feed my esophagus
with the cries of the homeless
the screams of the children of Palestine
campesinos of Chiapas
a reverb of Sandino
speeches of Che
ahimsa of Gandhi

I'll wrap their souls around my tongue
to strengthen my thoughts, they showed me
what it is to sacrifice for love

words will be bullets fired in the night
a molotov cocktail thrown at a tank
a rock in my defense

my voice will rise to shatter every misogynistic
statement ever spoken
a roaring Assata
a yelling Goldman
a shouting Lolita

I'll be the last breath of Anthony Baez
the last scream of Albizu
the final proclamation of Malik Shabazz
the last screech of Jimi's guitar
before he meets you on the other side

For when I cradle the title poet
I will know the truth
speak Armenian to tell you of our genocide
scat like Langston
Howl like Ginsberg
Love like Neruda
5 in the afternoon, Garcia Lorca said

I'll shake your hand firm to show my sincerity
I'll wish you shalom and utter the words of Celan
futurist Akhamatova
middle passage Sanchez,
black magic Baraka poetry
sandinista cardenal was our marx of victory

love will be my box of ammunition
haikus will be grenades in the hands
of children defending their homes
our skins, our elegies
our blood, our laments

my breath iambic intertwined with hope
this is a shriek, a groan, a grunt
a ballad, a sonnet, an ode
poems will be earthquakes in this infrastructure
paragraphs will be jabs in the face of capitalism

When I cradle the title poet
I will know what it is to love
because I know in its purest form
poetry is revolutionary
just like love

Pieces of my tiny soul

Unbreakable I
want my heart to be as strong
as my bones can be

Impenetrable
my sarcasm is my shield
from all the women

Indestructible
my body is worn thin from
all the four seasons

Interrogated
I was under hot lights for
all of my actions

She's heavy on the soul
not a burden
more like a planet to hold

She's light on the mind
feather talk conversations
of clouds and colors

Recuperating
my soul has been to hell and back
one thousand times

Life is made up of
a cycle of constant I
love you's and hate you's

I wish I could be
reborn, removed, re-booted
with a new program

a crash in my time
sixty obsolete minutes
I'm reinvented

The Creed of a Graffiti Writer
for TCK, FSH, NVS, 2DX, URN, WAS, 5MH

We strike at night
the streets of New York
is our canvas
we hide in the shadows
when the pig patrol strolls by
the moon gives us
our only source of light

We are the addicts of aerosol
the Krylon can clan
the Rustoleum patrol

We are the German tips spraying
backpack wearing
black book carrying
magnum pilot tagging
the wack toy buffers

We are the brigade of bombers
mounting on our midnight mission
of colorized madness
the color blending, spray paint
and mind melding maniacs

We are the ghetto Picassos
the modern day Matisses
the artistic Shakespeares
who tear white walls in half

We are the street canvas killers
with one quick splat of an ultra flat black
with silver outlines and yellow highlights
perfected during 3 A.M. skylines

We are the crews
that redecorate building walls
with wild styles burning
people's imagination
with motions of the can
the walls wail words of life
through sight of Krylon colors

On the streets of New York
we bomb city blocks
rocking throw ups on top of
windowsills while standing
on top of garbage cans

We are the ones who set
Bronx-Brooklyn expeditions
in the tradition of nomads
we go where no man's can
has sprayed on walls before

Our names are found
on high rises, bridges and building roofs
our plans are waterproof,
shockproof and foolproof

We are the tye dye tone tint marauders
who write manifestos on black walls
with Silver Unis, SG-7s and white Pentel markers

We mark the many lands and train stations
our tags ragged black books and cardboard
scratched on windows and train doors
stickers slapped over any
wack toy you had a beef with
but only in self-defense

We gaze at our glossy words
and lose ourselves in arrows
and 3-D shadows

We are the 12oz prophets
writing prophecies with our hieroglyphics
that help humans understand us

It is simply the love of seeing
our names on the wall
it is the symbolic value of feeling important
in a world we are lost in
It is the outlet that introduces art
into our way of thinking

We wear baggy jeans, baseball caps
and army fatigues
when we venture on our trip of
blending bombing wonderland

The street is our canvas
when art brushes and stencils don't matter
only Liquitechs and spray paint
the toxic aroma that enters our bloodstream
on nights when our fingertips freeze
writing upside down with the can
trying to get all the paint out

Feel the wrath of Graff .
when society calls us vandals and delinquents
that's why your child wants to be just like us

We bomb your door to tell you our name
it's a shame they've erased
our high rise artistic trains

the Far Rockaway-Lefferts A
the outside D, B and Q in Brooklyn
the Coney Island F
the Canarsie-Broadway Junction L
the J, M, and the Z
over the Williamsburg Bridge
the N and the R in Astoria, Queens
the 1 and the 9 in Washington Heights
the 2 and the 5 in the Bronx
the New Lots 3
the Jerome 4
the Westchester 6
and the Flushing purple 7 train

Now we rain on your law
the ink scribes scribble
on your forehead and pronounce you
Hip-Hoppily dead

the 4th son of Hip-Hop
overshadowed by Technic table microphones
and Puma's gray suede complexion tone

There is no Hip-Hop
without graffiti, only rap
so we wrap our hands
around cans becoming one

Our motions are studied
by plagiarist anthropologists
making money off our art

The spirits on clean canvas
can be hazardous to minds
when eyes can't understand
the buck wild style alphabet

Sunrises call for travels
homeward bound
We're the ones who make
the click clack click clack sound
with the can on new land
when a tag could get us shot

We are the artistic poets
who perform magic with spray paint
and just call ourselves writers
Graffiti writers.

Fela

mother had me on her back
a workhorse for my benefit

mother had my back
even with the benefit of doubt

mother held my hand firm
my backbone strength

mother had a firm hand
struck with force across my face

mother raised me alone
single like the sun

mother watched me grow
a flower in her hands

her only son
my only mother

the only sun
the only moon

birthed from her womb
a gift in the fall

our lives
our tombs

her struggle
my profit

my accomplishments
her reward

love for my mother
uncanny.

Boleros Blvd

Caribbean blue skies with sparkling nights
Havana has a silhouette of Che in the stars
an old Cuban lady reminds me of lightning bolts
the men whisper thunder
Cabio Sile, la comida para Chango

hearts wave their patria
the statue of José Martí looks exquisite
the sun on my back leaves streaks for memory
the salt air whirls off the coast of many sunsets

I can still hear the bombs of playa Giron
the plane crashing in Cienfuegos
the songs of bearded men

the smell of cigars
aqui en Santa Clara
I stare at the dreams
of el Comandante Che!

25 Years In

The future of past memories
a complex simpleton
a walking paradox
sleeping beauty never to awake
trying to find princess charming

A neon wilderness
a movable feast
the bastard child of Nuyorican poetry
a Garcia Marquez character drowning in light
a Camus character blinded by sand
Neruda's tiny captain of a valiant corpse
and Lorca's watch when it strikes 5

A rock and roll Puerto Rican
Hendrix's machine gun solo
the walrus, the crazy diamond,
and the karma police
a funky Stax bass line,
play that shit, Duck, play that shit,
old school Fania All-Stars salsa Aguanile
Dylan's nasal delivery
Coltrane's main vein
and ten percent of Thom York's voice
because ten percent is better than zero

BDP's The South Bronx, The South South Bronx
Common's I used to love her
a break beat that's recycled through
with 90's grunge, 60's psychedelic,
and Hip Hop's native tongues

Picasso's Guernica
Dali's melting clocks
Frida's body cast
and Basquiat's copyright symbol

A New York City skyline
jealous of cocks and towers
a 5 borough accent standing on
the corner of Milwaukee and Evergreen
in front of the magenta door

Center of attention deficient disorder
the D train turnstile hopper, the walkman,
the headphones, the music and the air guitar

A retired Graff piece
an empty spray can, a homemade marker
a funk super hero, a top city king
and one of 5 million hoods

Jesus, Slash, Weird Al,
Side-Show Bob and B-Real all in one

A missing member
of Bone Thugs and Harmony
In the punch line of every
long hair joke made after 1995
An extra on Welcome Back Kotter
the leader of The Black Guerilla Army
Vatos Locos! We live forever!

Insecure
A Puerto Rican whose not
Puerto Rican enough for others
Puerto Rican
standing in between

an Obituary and Nigger-Rican blues
trying to find a place

Not the same hands
who write poems at 17
A gain, A loss
A growth, A mourn
and actually moving out
of New York

Knowing there's ways to go as a poet
miles to walk before being tired
Not a black panther or a young lord
Not Che Guevara or Carlos Santana
Who people don't think as a hippie or a beatnik
anymore but now they think is Indie
because he wears Chuck Taylor's and old
looking clothes that cost 5 bucks
that he paid fifty for.

Not sure if poems are Bonafide
or Bonafide are poems?

Still dreaming, Still loving,
Still crying, Still growing,

Still seems harder than ever
bills have names on them
and have started to cradle
the word responsibility

It's been 10 years since
father has walked back into life
starting to learn to talk to him
and beginning to love the name Rojas

Still the same scared child
who writes poems in
black books instead of drawings

Poetically inclined
with an artistic mindset
genuine, original, authentic,
Bonafide

Blood and Tooth

In the old days
you would've been
the one thing we would've fought for
blood and tooth

Now you're another reason why we hate it
when people go mainstream
you seem disheveled
confused, walking around
people whispering in your ear
that it's all about you
what happened
to keeping your side of the bargain
remember your promise
to stay true or stay away

and since that day
we haven't seen you
they've heard about the little cameos you make
and the crowd you've been hanging with
is totally different from high school

Remember when you had style
everyone looked at you
the vanguard, the innovator
you were fresh

Now you're just another generic production
of American fashion with its tendency to suck
the life out of something new

Once in a while
we see little hints of the person we once knew
but usually all we see

are the puppet strings dangling
up and down for a few dollars
in commercials for alcohol
last time we checked you didn't drink

Remember when all we used to do
was talk about what we would do
if one of us ever made it
       fund a revolution
       open a bookstore
       a community center
and make sure no one ever jerks us around

Look at you now
a depressed millionaire with legions of fans
who don't even know your real name
Hip Hop, tell them your name

show them your potential
lead that revolution we talked about
to hell with corporate sponsorship
remember grassroots movements
jazz and blues
Malcolm and Fidel

the last poets told us once
that niggers are scared of revolution
show them you're not a nigger, Hip Hop
show them your love and passion
show them the cultural expression of inner city streets
show them NYC in the 70's, 80's, and 90's
contorted into one backspin whirlwind freeze
show them the murals in your heart of dead MC's
who were once the voices of the ghetto
poets who moved minds of every breathing
young human being

show them your bilingual rhyme
in Spanish, French and Japanese

remember the b-boys who taught you how to break
when you learned how to rock steady
and wore that turntable like a backpack
everywhere you went
you were a modern day blues man with guitar

Hip Hop,
What happened to you?
Was the money that tantalizing?
Did you buy everything you ever wanted?
Did it make you happy in the end?

At night, we tell stories of
how you showed us how to write
how to hop the trains, how to dress
how to explore different kinds of music

but now we are embarrassed
you're walking around like
you did everything by yourself

you were the only thing
we would've ever fought for
blood and tooth

Now you're another reason why we hate it
when people go mainstream

The truth

broken bodies the severed head
politicians the walking dead

invasion America's birth
genocide's gift the waking breath

hanging trails at town square meetings
burning crosses the children are bleeding

machines roll through cities, propaganda
crushes all who disagree with the agenda

brainwashed minds praise the dollar
capitalist the puppet scholar

inquisition, students of the cloth
pray to sin from greed to sloth

pilgrimages, twilight of the idol places
imprinted in minds the rise of dead faces

the truth is dead bodies been hung
buried alive without their tongues

the words are read, hidden is the truth
the minds are dead buried alive, like forgotten youth

Poetry

The beauty of words
bloom through the voice
giving birth to syllables
and conversations between
two people

Poetry

Flying skies with kites
blowing in the wind
a little boy riding
his bike down a hill

Poetry
a bowl of strawberries
a red balloon
a birthday present
a love letter
a baby's smile.

Poetry
the growth of my child
       depression
       loneliness
       politics
       music
       love
       death.

Life birthed on paper is poetry,
the movements of the ocean,
a sea breeze
a forest whisper
a mother laughing

a sister crying
a dog licking you in the face.

The offspring of the imagination
I was reincarnated
from past poets' souls
walking slowly

once Basho
once Pablo Neruda
once Arthur Rimbaud
once Julia de Burgos
once e.e. cummings
recitation of haikus
cantos and odes
drunken boat
yo soy negro poems

once Jimi Hendrix
playing my stratocaster upside down
red house on the hill
machine gun bullets that kill
singing about castles made of sand

once John Lennon
playing white pianos
mother never left me
imagination free

once Miles Davis
sketching blue fusion brew
dark magus of jazz
the coolest of the bop

Poetry is
a waterfall splashing
warm Puerto Rico rain drops
singing like Billie Holiday

The beauty of life listening
to the beauty of words
whispering in the wind.

Sonnet XXVII

Clamped in a tough metropolis
ahead with ease over suburbia
the sun quotes hot flashes
over oceans and lakes
trees and the north wind, nature
calls for the baptism of your
soul, attached to metal's grip
a use of vices, metamorphosis
iron butterflies in concrete jungles
a little rock speaks of landslides
exaggeration of such a young child
run wild in the wilderness
run naked in your life
mother nature is calling for your baptism.

Relaxers and Perms

**Rock and Roll is my religion
and I am a disciple of the distortion pedal
octaves, fuzz faces, 100-Watt Marshall stacks**

Rock and Roll Puerto Rican

Rock and Roll Puerto Rican

I am the illegitimate son
of rock and roll
the son of fender stratocasters,
Gibson Les Pauls,
Precision Basses and Flying V's

From Robert Johnson Delta Blues
to Muddy Waters Chicago
To the King of Kings
B.B. to Freddie to Albert
born under a bad sign
We got T-Bone, Hooker, Little Richard boogaloo
Booker T and the MG's green onion
melting pot grooves
To the funk of Eddie Hazel, Jimmy Nolen
Bootsy Collins, Larry Graham
To me this has always been black music
and will always be black music

my childhood consisted of Hendrix
psychedelic electric churches, red houses
and soul sacrificing Santana of Europa
jingo gypsy eyes, sambas and black magic women

Only Puerto Rican on my block
to blast bass drum kicks of Zeppelin
the genius of the Beatles
from eight days of yesterday
to a strawberry field revolution of Sgt. Pepper

The loud decibels of The Who,
bass lines of spiders and blind boy pinball wizards
the war pigs of Black Sabbath

evil women, iron men and chopped fingertips
in this wicked world

lunacy's landscapes on the dark side of the moon
run like hell, roger, run like hell
your mother's going to tell you if you're crazy or not

1994: 17 year old hip hop head with
Hendrix, Miles and Marley on the wall
And I have friends who ask,
"Yo B, where's the hip hop?"
Raised on Public Enemy, a Tribe called Quest
De la Soul and Nas' first Album
Their shine still lasts longer than most

but the guitars and drums of rock and roll
always captivated me so much more
John told me he was the walrus
Jimi showed me his anguish that is Machine Gun
David played his solo in Comfortably Numb
Freddie was the glamour of Bohemian Rhapsody
Thom wailed his insanity on Paranoid Android
Anthony sang melancholy Under the bridge
And Kurt said the riff to Smells like teen spirit
was a straight Pixies rip off

Rock and roll for me was my way out
My musical representation of lunatics,
drunks, drug addicts and overdosed icons
asphyxiated by their own vomit
shotgun blasts to their heads
praise the dead for their music
so their voices can be heard

OK computers and Evil Empire
Signs of the times using your illusion

8 minute opuses of a woman named Layla
like Oedipus overtures called The End

pentatonically boxed
with calloused hands breaking headstocks
smashing amps and sacrificing guitars
to the gods who made love

Rock and Roll is my religion
and I am a disciple of the distortion pedal
octaves, fuzz faces, 100-Watt Marshall stacks
and a Vox wah-wah
obsessed with buying guitars
with every paycheck

my mother would ask me
how could I love the Beatles and Wu-Tang
so much and at the same time
I explained it's the same
as her loving salsa and doo-wop
big sister's loving r & b and house music
each generation creates its own love for music
and I know I love rock and roll
and Yes, I'm Puerto Rican too.

Tunnel Visions
for the homeless of the NYC Transit System

Death has the upper hands on humanity
life was left with a wild man's lunacy
curiosity killed the cat and the Homosapiens
and left the dogs of war to rule the world

The train, mobile homes for hobos
homeless musicians and victims asking for change
got stabbed bloody ribcage
express to 59th Street

Town prophets reciting the bible
ripping the pages out
people use them as gum wrappers
prophets stoned by the passengers

Hobo plays his drum with wife
he repeats the same lines every time
I see them, she plays the bass drum
old hollow boxes of dreams

Liberty, an absent plea
in people's minds
more obsessed with
the thoughts of capitalism.

Burned buildings the view
from Burnside's platform the Dominican restaurant
is still open, 3 dollar dish specials
but the train is coming maybe it's open later.

Shakespeare is on the corner
lip-synced by beautiful lips
no one can hear her

but I know it's Henry the fifth.

el barrio, lands of flags and pride
smack middle in the capital of the world
riots and roses, death and daisies,
murals and memories
god and a garden in between 1st and 2nd avenues

The hobos have animosity towards death
because it's more peaceful
and it's like a silent movie
all's quiet and peaceful when your eyes are closed.

Ode to Ricardo

Tell me Ricardo
How were you as a child?
you told me you lost your mother
at an early age

spoke highly of your father
a railroad operator
trips with him
was that your early fascination
with nature?

you turned these images
into maternal themes
Was that for your mother?

you cradled love at an early age
sang songs of despair
I sang those same songs with you
dozens of times

Tonight I am writing you
a letter 8 years overdue
How were you as a young man?
you accepted the college road
going to the capital
still writing down your bones and branches

Melodies of what life offered you
then you traveled the way young writers love to,
I've lived vicariously through you

Late in your 20's
In the Far East
with a beast called loneliness

Josie bliss in at your existence
poems for angels and odes with laments

Ricardo, tell me about Spain
How was it when you were there?
An ant exposed Marxism in art
Federico taught you to enjoy life
until your last breath
and Alberto Rojas Jimenez came flying

your residence I've followed you
every inch of the way
from the Far East to Spain
to France to Mexico back to Chile
I followed your every move

Then you started to sing
sing a grand song
that would only be echoed
by revolutions in Latin America
twenty years later
your song rang in every writer's ear
to whoever wanted to write their own history

And what of your wives?
Has poetry always been her
or a mistress on the side?
you've written odes and cantos
laments and sonnets
love and war
life and loneliness
death and joy

Ricardo
Why do you think your father
wouldn't have been proud of you?

changing your name to spare his pride
that his son was a poet and
not a real working man
taking names of german writers
and common campesino names
you've done things that no one's done before
your father lays his pride on your shoulders
and I rest my inspiration
upon the enormous gorge that is you
a man named Ricardo
but the children call you Neruda

Daily Rituals

The time is 8 a.m.
a new day is born
and at the crack of dawn
gunshots fire
Pop! Pop! Pop! Pop!
I awaken from my sleep
bullets fire through my window
through my flag
and into my living room wall

I get up
wash my face, brush my crooked teeth
back, forth, get dressed
and start walking the street
picking my hair out
no birds outside
I live in the ghetto
birds migrate permanently

not me
I love where I live
phone company down the block
pizza dollar shop on every street
bodegas on every corner
jibaros play capicu in front
of the building with their guayaberas on
"mira, steven, cuando te vas a cortal ese pelo?"
nunca, never, no way

graffiti on every wall
muralists design heaven's hall
in a handball court
time keeps on ticking and
I hit the street eye boggled, eyebrows raised

sunlight's rays shine through my hair
and their eyes follow my head bopping
like bouncing balls and I continue walking
from my initial destination

because it's 12:43
and in 5th period English
and teachers babble on blackboards with
chicken scratch handwriting telling me
"to get an education"
"school is cool "
"crack is wack"
"education is the key to the future"

true
but with million dollar spokespeople
never setting foot on my rundown
paint chipped asbestos of a learning ground
replaying their catch phrases over and over
to sink into our minds
like an Orwellian subliminal message
"How am I supposed to take them seriously?"

my contemplation of thoughts
continue wandering through the streets
back and forth fifth, sixth and seventh avenues
all I see is poverty stricken neighborhoods
kids wander the alleyways like rats
wearing rag tag worn out hand-me-downs
but that's just one of the problems my eyes see
police messing with every Tyrone, Malik,
Juan, Papo, Jose, Steven, Marlon, Dwayne Wayne
and even Mr. Jefferson he lives on the east side
116th and Lexington Ave.
even he gets harassed in my neighborly hood

One day I got harassed
"Put your hands on your head!"
the police officer shouted
and I put my hands on my head
"Put your knees on the floor!"
he shouted again and I said
       "What! I just bought these jeans yesterday
       $67.00 dollars these pants cost me and I'm not
       messing them up on this nasty ass floor"
"What did you say boy!" badge number 5150 said
pointing his .45 magnum in my face
       "At this point in time sir
       I'm experiencing major
       back problems, so bending my knees would
       be hazardous to my health"
The next minute
I'm thrown on the floor with the pig screaming
"DON'T MOVE OR I'LL SHOOT YOUR STUPID ASS!"
and I'm thinking to myself
Why are you screaming? I'm on my stomach.
 What am I going to do? Roll away!

as he frisks me he uses his non-pronunciation
Spanish 101 failure wannabe bilingual accent

"Where you going Mr. Roegass," he asked
       "That's Rojas, sir," I said
"Whatever, all you damn spics have
the same thousand last names anyway," he snickered

"Do you have any cousins named
Rodriguez, Hernandez, Fernandez or Ortiz?
Oh wait! What about Colon or Rivera?
You must have a cousin or two dozen
with the name Rivera," he rambled

"No," I said
"So where were you going?" he asked again
"I'm going to my cousin's house," I said
"Which one?" he laughed with the smell of
pork rinds oozing out of his mouth
"Someone reported a gun firing and the man
fits your complexion…, uh I mean description,"
he said with a smirk

still on the hard South Bronx streets
I'm a 6 foot light skin Puerto Rican brother with an afro
if I had a gun would I even let you stop me
let alone throw me on the floor, spit in my face,
fuck up my pants, mispronounce my name,
make fun of my family, etc., etc., etc…

they let me go just another case
of mistaken identity real stories of
the south Bronx patrol
it's 6 o'clock
Check the sun positions shadows
overhead my eyebrows
I pick my hair out, play air guitar
eyes continue to boggle
people mesmerized by my 90's afro
one brother said, "right on"
I told him, "Wrong decade"

check my watch the time is 6:43 p.m.
when I look up there's a crowd staring at me
shouting questions and statements

"YOU'RE AN ABOMINATION TO HUMANS!"
they screamed
No I'm not I replied
"ARE YOU WHITE?"

they asked
No I said
"YOU CAN'T BE PUERTO RICAN!"
they screamed again
 but I am I told them
"ARE YOU A HIPPIE?"
No I said, getting frustrated
"IS YOUR HAIR A WIG?"
No it's not I said
"YOU KNOW YOU LOOK LIKE JESUS?"

ignoring the mob I continue
walking the street and after picking my hair
a thousand times, I reach my home of rest
eat, sleep, shit
read, relax, relate
release, maintain
and end my daily ritual.

Bonafide Rojas

Euphoria's tango

A tango in the clouds
A mango in your dreams
A labyrinth of soul, one million
doorways that lead to you

A pillow, cotton picked cloud
resting your eyes in your dream
your body running through a
million shades of light of you

Euphoria was her name
I enjoyed chasing her
until my legs were broken

Euphoria, she laid in the shadows
as I looked for her in the light
and she opened another door
and disappeared.

Basquiat

So tell me   Jean Michel?

How did it feel to be pedestalized
then pick-a-ninnied, 1982
a Haitian Puerto Rican
in a pop art world on a raft by yourself,
war holed in galleries in Munich, L.A. and Tokyo
but what about The Lower East Side
the same old song of SAMO
slogans tell your life on brick walls of Loisaida

Lithographs, wood, canvas cutouts
sketched with black marker Pilots
house painted your devotion for
Dali and Picasso
showing your true colors for your heroes
Charlie Parker, Joe Louis,
Muhammad Ali and Roberto Clemente

How did it feel   Basquiat?

Being the only black man, Graffiti writer
Turn talk of the art world in less than a year
From chalk floors to oils
jessoed in basement studio spaces
with hills of cocaine next to buckets of white paint
you tried to stay sane
inherited the love for the moment
in these days of excess
addicted to painting your torture
breaking your bones   slowly
breaking your spirit   slowly
but all you wanted to do was paint

your soul on the street and be a little famous
to paint your acid tripped LSD on anything

then you were tapped by
art gallery dealers who represented you
wheeled and dealed for you
but did they have your voice, your interest
they knew they could make a lot of money
off you and they slaved you
Your output was phenomenal
dozens of paintings
flying out of your hands at the hands
of these dealers who dealt pieces of
your soul to people who just wanted
a piece of the hype

then it's your relationship
with Warhol   .   Jean Michel
Your collaboration with the
Intergenerational pop icon
who was inspired by your energy
I know you idolized Andy
The one man who embodies contemporary
You desperately wanted his approval
You two were inseparable
working and partying together

Warhol never joined you
in your escapades of drugs
but he watched you in your youthful abrasiveness
Was he sincere in telling you he liked your paintings?
Or did he snicker the way he did?
Was he man enough to say you
had more raw untapped energy than he ever would?

Did he   Jean Michel?

Warhol built you up
then broke you down
A white pimp with a black painting whore
in a downtown art scene
made of leeches and snakes
painting their lives away

Who's using who
in this power dynamic
struggle of race and culture
Who's using who
27 years of your life fresh and vibrant
you had dozens and dozens of years
to paint your heart out to show people
what it meant to be a painter, a black painter

Tell me   Basquiat?

How does it feel
to be a tainted immortal in an art world
that whispers under its breath
and says all you did was scribble
But you inspired me to paint
and paint slogans of poverty
and anti-capitalist lines over America's dream
of art imitating life
showed me to paint with a marker
draw on doors, sketch on the subway
showed me that graffiti is ART

It's the same old song
It's the SAMO song

Tell me   Jean Michel
How does it feel?

Deja vu

I have seen love
in the forms of angels and knights
silver masks floating in bodies of water
and until dawn's race begins again
I stand on mountaintops touching stars
and believing in god

sending saints wrapped in
human form to walk on the earth's name
for enemies to hold to kiss under bloody moonlight

seductions and suicides
I've seen it undeniably
with a rose's thorns pricked
and held in my hand with blood dripping
giving the ground life and giving me faith

for I have seen love in the form of death
in the form of suicides and hangings
where the sun never shines his ego on
the moon crying and holding jealousy
in between her bosom

stars laughing and taunting her heart
fragile like a crystal love to fill
to be felt through her body
with the sight of whom
she cherishes under the clouds
dancing to the music of life

air fluttering in her lungs
golden butterflies when the saints walk
the land like mortals

she too will fall in love with something mortal

devotion waits by the gates
I wait for love to come back for me

I've seen heaven in her skin
her face carved by an angel
when I die spread my ashes across the sky
so I can kiss her body

for I have seen love
in the forms of suns and moons.

The Epic of Abca:
A sun named Abca

Abca stares at the hands
of the eye of the beholder
holding nothing
but the astros

at last
the beginning began
when she blinked
the third eye was
the first eye and

he is the sun
of the first sky
son of the first space
inhabitant at
the palace of praise

he is the trumpeter
who blows on
the eve of Armageddon

he, cloud dancer
who waltzes and
tangos with time
and picks mangos
off the tree of knowledge
never apples
apples alter his appetite and
poison his presence

Omni ever flowing
hair ever growing
into deep space

nine children
He has that revolve around
himself and he ciphered
himself in the flame and
calls this place milky way
because the stars sway
back and forth
to the beat box he creates

It causes black holes
and worm holes
the sounds flow
like Venus rain
smoothly through
silver skies and
copper clouds

rides on the backs of
golden tan tortoises
watching caterpillar metamorphosis
into butterflies mating
with dragonflies
birthing butter-dragons
flying the skies with
rainbow colored wings
that land on his eyelids
so he may see life in color

he is the eccentric eclectic
who recites epitaphs in forms
of echoes that bounce from
children's ears to elder's ears
and it takes years of travel
so when the elders hear
it's time to move on

The beholder gave birth to
two prodigies that
manipulate molecules and
manifest knowledge for he
is the gardener of the tree
and the other one created
seconds, minutes and hours

mother stands outside of reality
her body is the universe
her name is eternity
she made the feelings of
euphoria an epidemic
she holds time
in her left hand and
Abca in her right hand and
time was a brother
he played with
every 24 hours
and when eternity blinked
time started again

he stares at the hands of
the eye of the beholder
holding nothing
but him and time and
she was outside of time
because she created time
and time creates
lives and deaths and

She gave birth to him and
the first thing he saw
were her hands and
he is the son of eternity
the sun of the universe and

brother to time

so now he dances on
stars and clouds
and lets time
take its course
while he shines.

The Epic of Abca:
Child of the cosmos

from the
song of his muse
came siren sounding
lyrics that entranced
his ears while he sits and listens

preparations for
enigmatic mystifying
rides of time travel
on the backs of
rainbow serpents

writing on skylines
while stars shined
on his face
leaving names
on the craters of the moon

residing on the blue side
the cool vibes side
cool monsoons spray
on the backs of lunar dancers
dancing in crystal cathedrals

still traveling
he stopped for a taste
of sunbeam waterfalls
off the coast of Venus beaches

birthed from the womb
of eternity
magnificent metamorphosis
from mortal to magician

of millions

transformation into hummingbird flocks
while clocks strike midnight
he takes flight, flying through clouds
arising in the dawn's rays
leaving footprints on mountains
riding Neptune's chariot of water
on 50 foot waves splashing into
sunsets and moonrises

children give surprises in
glory boxes
unlocking vocal harmonic
sounds that break syllables
during soliloquies of solitude

the muse's magic
mesmerized mind states
when she whispered
in the wind revealing
worlds inside worlds

her words were watched
by wise owls in
the hour of the night
he surfed on voiceless screams
of his own in space

sleepless dreams laced
in asteroid belts and then
a star appeared on the left eye
of his face, child of the cosmos
Abca was called

he meditated on Mars and
break danced on top of Jupiter

he seduced women on Saturn
and stole the rings for his daughter

he plundered Pluto and
sold ice across the galaxy
mostly for a five dollar fee

he tanned on
the sun's outer flare
bare on the
mountains of Mercury
bathed on the banks of
the blue river of Uranus

recited poetry for nymphs
in the oceans of Neptune

wrote epics on top of Earth's
Mt. Everest for the attention
of her eyes

he captured stardust for a
present for my muse
her words made worlds
revolve and now he sits
while she sings songs that
make stars sparkle.

The Epic of Abca:
The death of time

time unwinds in
the arms of his mind
lines himself with invisible vines
led into signs of sublime sounds

hypnotic rivers surround
dry mounds hugging the sands
with their wet lips
dreams floating above

the trees underneath the sky
the sun's eye blinks
blue oceans eclipse with clouds
nature's aroused by

the blend of her two children
her eternal ecstasy
exercises energies
for a utopian tendency

beautiful reflections
a room full of mirrors
a sun's selection of stars
to shine on him

a flower enjoys solitude
beside puddles of water
silence is golden
like his mother's eyes

when she smiles
he takes a tulip
to the one who captured

his eyes and soul

offered his/my devotion
whispers walk with the wind
each step taken slowly
the world spins on its axis

the moon is envious of
the sun but loves Venus
because the earth is too blue
for sunshine

times are unwinding while
spiders are spinning their homes
the earth is spinning
time's ticking alone

hanging seconds
with invisible vines
reading the signs
drowning in sound aloud

dying in the sands
sleeping in the sky
the sun's eye blinks again
time is hanging minutes

with see-through strings
ignoring the signs
swimming in noise
buried in beaches

a tree stands there
with its roots being
sucked by leeches
time hurts like death

a game of forever
tick tock hung them
with transparent vines
because they didn't read

the signs that told them
of the songs of sublime sounds
and continued to walk into the
river of stillness and was

introduced to nature, she
told time that time is ending
suicide is the foreseen outcome
so nature let time experience love before time

hung seconds and then hung
himself with invisible vines
silence is golden and
the world is still spinning
on its axis.

The Epic of Abca:
The Elder

Growth into elders
old age comes experience
wise eyes see old memories
flash in Abca's mind
like the earth
living and dying
watching mountains
flash in and out of reality
transparent blocks
on the streets of invisibility

gardens grow on the
palms of his hand
open blooming, closed death
need sunlight to grow
wrinkled hands
have rivers flowing through it
forests seeded in his mind
birthed from his voice

last of his kind
like his soul
last of its kind
living and dying
landscapes of streets
of nothingness
trees raised on the
bones of Abca's back

spine broken
from the weight
of the world
legs shattered

from walking the nine planets
north   south   east   west

old boys Abca's legs are
he's seen a billion sunsets
and a million new moons
and each time it was different
standing on a mountain
sunshine bathing
moonlight serenades
hands are crippled
from the picking of roses
thorns on my soul
pricking at my sanity
drowning in drops of water

chills from drafts of shadows
sun never rises on the
darkness of permanent night
stones whisper to the wind
traveling
to the mountains
telling secrets of travelers
who used to walk on the land

dandelions laugh at
the shore of the sea
sea breezes wander
splashing waves smashing
castles made of sand
breaking his thoughts
underwater reefs
raindrops fill empty holes
on his back nurturing back to health
nature's childish water
plays on Abca's hair

making it damp

fields giggle when
the sun is lowering
outside his eyesight
he'd captured light in a bottle
and stored it for
the time of night
the hills have inscripted
epitaphs of people
he once knew
plateaus hold poems
written on the planet's face
his rocking chair faces the ocean
the oceans of slaves
the oceans of ships
that invaded the land
he walks on
that he takes care of

Abca
the last of his kind
walking alone
his soul
the last of its kind

the sunsets
once again
one billion and one
and a new moon is born

Abca
caretaker of the world
gardener of the land
walks alone.

The Epic of Abca:
1000 year-old winds

the wind blows
1,000 year-old breaths
with rocking chair patience
clouds shaped from the
eyesight's imagination
sunlight's sensation

a bird's autumn migration
companions

the scent of her stayed on Abca
the smell of her lotion skin
the distinct curl of her hair
rubbing the remains of her
on his skin

his touch was really her touch
Abca walks off the mountain
into the sun's flame
whispering her name across the sky
the clouds form ears
to show him something is listening
he breathes

stands on top of rock islands
throwing pieces of his soul into the ocean
watching them sink
each one a letter in her name
broken heart pieces
seven times he wanted to say

"I would die for you"

Abca watches
the sun's flame dies out
watching the moon be born again
swallow the moonshine
desperately trying to find
pieces of her soul

so he could put her back together
replace the empty space
like the 1000 year-old winds
he travels the planet as it rotates
he watches the birds
form animal empires in the sky

Abca's eyes stare at the reflection
infinite sadness
the sand impersonated her facial shape
her nose, her lips, her eyebrows
her hair has vines and stardust in them
her beauty comparable to the blue sea
divine and gentle
melancholy and sincere
oceans are bodies
her eyes are islands
in white water
and blue land

Abca bathes in her scent and
exhales his existence
The time of birds are coming
The sun is born again
The clouds are gone

breathe a memory
Abca breathes in 1000 year-old winds
unwinding in the arms of time

1000 memories flash in and out
hauled on my back, a game of atlas
dressed in cosmic suncloth
tailor made by her memories
stitched with her hair

his eyes laid low from the bright light
her soul is sunshine
the sight frightened me
Abca sleeps in the night
showed him the light
guided by her memories
experience to swallow

Abca breathes new winds with
new time and new memories
reborn through her
the place is new
like a baby exiting the womb
this place is new
everything is born
Abca exhales his first memory
A one year-old wind.

Invisible Ones
for Pedro Pietri

we talked
we walked
we bought
we fought
we lived
we died
we are the ones
with accents in conversations
who get passed by on every street
as something else
urban jibaros
questions of skin complexion
light or dark
¿De donde eres?

we who are
in the middle of every discussion
of race relations because we are dark light
Spanish English speaking tongues
broken dialects to go with broken dreams

we who were
fed images of false equal opportunities
and non-green carded citizenship
capitalism and congressmen
put us all in the arms of big brother
the stranglehold of IRS taxes

we who are
cursed by machismo
love salsa and merengue
battled for self respect and our independence
considered second-class citizens

a prize of war of bloody Sundays
radiation treatments
bombed Vieques and bombed Bushwick
gentrified Harlem and justice rallies

your existence we protested
and you fired your utensils of death
on children, women and men
all dressed in white

Invisible

we who breathe
the same polluted air
the same infectious water
pray to the same gods
sit by each other on the same train
eat food in the same places
listen to the same music
attend the same schools

but are always in the middle

trapped in the television of life
that's black and white
never believed in Technicolor dreams
only in the color of green
underpaid and overslaved
sweatshops and chop shops
in a schizophrenic American dream

Invisible

we who fight
over which island is better than which
on New York Streets

speaking colonized English
instead of colonized Spanish
and fight over who has
better food, better music,
better ball players and better cars
(which are either American, Japanese,
or German made)

never understood that we're all from a history
that has neglected us
transformed us from savage Indians
to 21st century Pepsi pop stars
and never cared for our culture
unless they can make a profit out of it
a media that bleaches the color
from our skin and believes
we all come with Eurocentic features
with English tongues

we have afros and dreads
straight hair, curly, kinky
black, blond, red hair
thin and thick lipped
brown eyes, blue, green
hazel contacted eyes
full spectrum of life rainbow's beauty
never understood
our full potential
for our darkness and brightness
we are the invisible ones

                we talk
                we walk
                we bought
                we fought

we lived
we died

but all we wanted was
to be seen, heard and respected
because we bleed
like everyone else.

Awakenings

Pigeons die on Easter
Resurrected the third day
To become kings

A Silent Waltz

a waltz, silent in the moonlight
ripe, moving through grape orchards
a mist surrounding body's curves
motion imprinted on sand

a waltz, careful in the arms of another
protected in each grasp of fingers groping
mandolins serenade the background music
of butterflies, a full moon, a voluptuous breast

a waltz in a time of disaster, where chaos is culprit
something as simple as a waltz
could make things better

sunrise, the sky grabs the hands of the sun
and dances across her body
until the sun leaves her again

Fades and Touch-ups

When the book comes out
I want you to sell it
to every doctor, nurse, guard
and cafeteria worker
who watched me grow up
in the hospital
and tell them
this is my son's blood, sweat,
tears and flat voice
singing in between these lines

In My Defense

Story of my accent

The weight of my tongue
stretched across
Generation's fingertips
rerouted in history's memory
 a second generation Puerto Rican

Transplanted in New York City
with grandparents having visions of grandeur
and hearing the stories of streets of gold
and opportunities to get out of Puerto Rico

Mother, aunt and two uncles
the baggage
Mother oldest of them all
played second surrogate parent
babysitter, Sister,
first one to work

When they first came
arrived the year 1952
86 & Amsterdam, Chelsea,
traveling uptown to 141st and Alexander
then 138th and Willis Avenue
right next to the 40th precinct, St. Jerome's Church
and the bar at the corner

Father: Miguel Rojas was left-handed
everyone called him "Lefty"
Mother's name Felicita
the spanish translation to Felicity

my first name Steven
Mother once told me
I was named after a baseball player

from the New York Yankees and
in 1977 I still have no clue
who was a popular baseball player
by the name of Steven
It could've been worse
My name could've been Thurman after Munson
and for a Puerto Rican kid from the Bronx
it would've been a burden
so Steven was a good choice

In fourth grade another Steven was in class
and the teacher started calling me Rojas
and pronounced it wrong every time
and until this day I still have problems
telling my whole name

Rojas in Spanish is red plural
and Steven means Crown in Greek

at early ages
I spent summers in Lomas Verde and Guanica
home at 175th and the Grand Concourse
early memories of black leather curtains
my uncle's house sitting back from vacation
and I tell my mother this story
but of course she snickers and says
"Ok, that's nice, Pop"
"You were four, right," still staring at the television

my youth
playground, toys in the plants
Nintendo, birthday parties
        New Year's Eve, always our house
        and the yearly Christmas dinner

I told my mother once
"What if I hit Santa in the head with a bat?
Would you be mad at me?"
She looked at me with those eyes the devil
would be proud of
I ran off hurrying into bed

My room, which I shared,
a half plywood-half sheetrock wall separated us
Mother had put up on her own with her bare hands
This was the sign for her fanaticism with
Martha Stewart and Christopher Lowell
I would discover years later

Sister's room was heaven
        the phone jack,
        the window, the door,
        natural sunlight
even the sheetrock was white

My room was hell
        brown plywood,
        gray painted walls, shadows,
        corners to put dirty clothes in
and a beat up old radio

At thirteen
I learned I could sleep with my headphones on
but she would still hear it banging on the wall
I would mumble some gibberish and try to fall asleep

my slurring of words
is a trait from childhood I picked up
by talking to myself
My truths sound like trooffs
My deaths sound like deafs

My pronunciation is jumbled with highly paced speech

Hip-hop infused with rock and roll
laced with political theory making love
to poetic structures and hanging out with
my boys on the corner,
that's where my tongue comes from

To my grandmother's loud and piercing voice
to my mother's cursing in two languages
fast enough to confuse a court stenographer?

To my father's repetitive nature and hard headedness
in thinking he's always right
to my sister's calm demeanor
switching to the Gemini monster
that I hated when I was young complaining
about everything and everything

To the memorization of Tribe called Quest Lyrics to
rage against the Machine
wailing to Jimi Hendrix whining to
memorization of Biggie lyrics to Led Zeppelin wailing to
Radiohead whining to just hanging with my family
That's where my accent comes from

Journal Entry: 9.13.01, Los Angeles, CA

My mom turned 51 today. 51 years of her loud brash attitude and she still sounds like a 22 year-old. We went to L.A. for her birthday, my family nucleus consisting of mother, daughter and I enjoying the hot humidity L.A. is known for, landed on the 8th. Last year we went to Paris and my mom couldn't stop saying Le Car Rouge, the double-decker tour bus name. In L.A., we saw the sights, Hollywood sign, Staples Center, Walk of Fame and The Chinese Mann Theatre. Mom has the tendency to see everything in two days and would leave the third if she could but we we're here until the 12th. On the 11th we got a phone call at 6 in the morning. My sister told my mother to turn on the TV. Turned it on and there was the sight of one of the Towers on fire. We sat there for 8 hours in bed watching news coverage on every station, hoping for something else to catch, a video to take me away from the madness I was nowhere near. I had my mother and sister with me, so I was partially calm. Thought about the employees at the Borders on the main level; I worked with many of them when I used to work there. I called people in Detroit, Chicago and tried NYC a dozen times but never got through. People didn't know what was going on; some were still sleeping. I started to think about everything I've read in the past couple of years of coup d'etats, invasions, blowbacks and understand if this is the karma the United States had created for itself. I calm my mother down who is starting to get upset. The scene of Middle Eastern people celebrating gets her really mad; she starts screaming at the TV. I tell her of stories I've heard about Palestine and the brutal war raging in the West Bank, and I explain that this scene could be from anywhere, anytime, where are the reporters, where's the date? They could be celebrating Allah's birthday twelve years ago and someone found it appropriate to show it now. She giggles as I try to explain

U.S. foreign policy and how they teach everyone to take down governments and invade other countries; well, spook sat by the door and this time walked through the front. My sister walks in yelling, "Are you watching?" TV still shows burning buildings. My sister and I try to explain the actions of the United States to my mother. From Guatemala to Nicaragua to Mexico to Puerto Rico to Indonesia to Iraq to Palestine to The Bronx to Brooklyn. We watch the TV without switching channels. The next day we start to worry because I left NYC with no proper ID. I lost my passport somewhere in between NYC, Chicago and back to NYC. At La Guardia, my mother and sister vouched for my existence with a social security card and a Xerox copy of my passport. Since coming back from Chicago with no hair, I look like Suheir's little brother. I'm worried. My sister says, "You're in it deep now; prepare for greyhound." I've always been told I look Middle Eastern and I cracked jokes about looking Arabic; now those jokes aren't funny. We were at a conference for my sister's job in L.A. and tagged along; weren't supposed to but for a cheap trip to L.A. I'm not saying no. Her job chartered a plane from Long Beach to New Jersey for the 86 employees of the east coast branch to leave on the 13th. On the morning of our departure my sister said that my mother and I are going to be able to fly back on the chartered plane. I was excited because a bus ride from L.A. to NY is about 4 to 5 days and I can't handle that. We left Long Beach around 1:00 pm, and we were on one of the only planes in the sky. We stopped in Lincoln, Nebraska, and my sister took a Valium and was talking gibberish and sounded as if she took a hit of ecstasy in the ladies room. In the air I enjoy the clouds and sun setting. I told myself that I'm glad that I was with mother and sister and if I die right now I'd be prepared because they're right next to me smiling. I kiss my mom on the forehead, wish her a happy birthday and tell her to get a nap, we're landing soon.

Dream Chasers

In between the pores
of immigrants' tongues
　　　lies the ability to
　　　create their own world

　　　In the exhales of their breaths
experience seeps through the cracks
of their teeth to tell stories of their motherland
indigenous uprising, and American backed coups

Images on silver screens
happy days of black and white memories
　　　motion picture soundtracks

To tell stories of
survival passed on from
ear　　　to　　　ear
　　　to griots to priests
　　　prophets who teach
　　　poets who inscribe epitaphs
on their foreheads

stories of crossing borders
rolling on the ground underneath barbwire
with fake birth certificates
traveling with black eyed angels
across oceans and rivers
government posts, rifles and helicopters
just to try to see what's
　　　　　　　on the other side
　　　　　　　because they heard stories
of streets paved with gold
Juxtaposed Christs
around necks to protect

haloes on their backs
"Por favor, madre, forgive me"
cultured shock and crossed boundaries
first time they've ever seen
skyscrapers and gringos

Their tongues branded the word
in the back of their cheeks to wait for years
to see who could recognize
speech that conjures spirits
sentences that cause pain
syllables that create euphoria.

Generations of the oppressed
will build new empires
in the throats of those who
will become the voices of the voiceless

In the pores of immigrant tongues
lie secrets that unlock
dreams to be free and equal
raising children in the belly of the beast
with open eyes in a dream corrupted

Sex chained the drug ring
transporting life in cocaine bags
sweatshop mosquitoes caught in a dream
that never existed for the people of the sun
knocking on the borders
trap doors the welcome mat
fall into the gap

Handcuffed to sewing machines
stitching blood in every pant and shirt
of the American design
noosed with Nike's laces

basket cased in the market place
their family is the target market,
their hands are the prime targets

Fields of glory
tainted whipping posts
underdeveloped stomachs pressed under
the leather of military boots
The fight to keep America
safe from new immigrants
INS keeps the fear intact

> *"Those who control the past control the future;*
> *those who control the present control the past"*

families' forgotten memories of immigrants
in a new land with gold rush fever and ghettos
in New York
descendants of a forgotten past
punish the present for the same action
as their family tree had committed
in search of the dream.

the sleeping giants
waiting for the sun to rise
in their eyes to show them their
dream is still alive
all they were doing
was chasing a dream.

In My Defense

I wanted to write a poem
you'll be proud of and ask your friends
if their sons had ever immortalized
them on paper with words

When friends ask,
"what do your children do for a living?"
you tell them, "My son's a poet," and after, you explain
that your daughter makes 100,000 dollars a year,
you tell them I am a self taught guitar playing bass
player, who's in a 2 man band, a Columbia university
dropout and a retired graffiti writer and you
tell them again, "My son's a poet"

I wanted to show you I meant what I said
that I wouldn't be like my father doing nothing in life,
I'm broke, yes but I'm doing something I love

We've talked about this before and yes
I'm going back to school, I know it's been 5 years
since my last college course
but when I go back I'll graduate, get a degree
and make you the proudest woman
alive for at least that one day

Every time someone says the words
poet, poem, poetry, I want you to think of me
and know that I always think of you
when I hear Pink Floyd's Mother, Fela Kuti
and rage against the machine's Bulls on Parade.
That's our wah-wah song

I want you to tell random people
that your son knows the difference
between sestina & sonnet, villanelle & canto,

haiku & calligram and when they look at you crazy
you'll know how I feel when I tell random people
those same exact things and they give me the same
exact looks, we're bonding

When the book comes out I want you to sell it
to every doctor, nurse, guard and cafeteria worker
who watched me grow up in the hospital
and tell them this is my son's blood, sweat,
tears and flat voice singing in between these lines

When friends ask,
"Why does your son write poems about you?"
You tell them because graffiti, rock and roll, and myself
aren't the only things I know to write poems on
your anger, attitude, pack rat syndrome &
schizophrenia are great points of inspiration
for and everything
that made you a great mother and great father

You can tell people that I make about 10,000 dollars
a year now. Teaching how to write poetry,
hating the establishment loving Neruda and Lorca,
Baraka and Sanchez,
and now not look so embarrassed
when you tell them I'm a poet,
you'll be embarrassed when you tell them
I'm a communist, if it gets to that point

And remember this is the only way
I know how to make you cry
and because my best poems are the ones
I write about you

Love, your Son
a kid named Bonafide

Plastic City
for Federico Garcia Lorca

Out in the city
sleepless nights
walks in the street
nocturnal lights
shine on Broadway

flicker sparks from
the garbage can fires
yellow oceans
taxicab waves splashing
unsuspecting pedestrians

the green, yellow
red lighted reflections
off the puddle on the ground
that shine on
the old man's face

preventing sleep
in his cardboard condo
ex-Vietnam veteran
war torn memories
social security didn't accept

god bless America
in the eyes of dead eagles
stamped on worthless
dead dollars
people kill and die for

obsessed for
monetary delights
infected by their monetary disease

working their whole lives
to strike it big

dreams fulfilled in new Cadillacs
wishes given to palm readers
addicted to slots and black jack
21 thousand times they have tried
lotto win for life jackpot

Atlantic City casino
Vegas adventures
and they come back
with their dreams shattered
and wishy washy like the memories

drowned in the rain of their tears
clouds of smoke
float over the city
skyscrapers dwarfing
the residential buildings

where life goes on
where the cycle spins
rapidly
big city blues
old paths walked

repetitions of screaming
once every   minute
repetitions of crying
once every   minute
repetitions of dying
once every   minute

New York City
the metropolis monster

running wild with worries
of others' worlds
but their own

staring at the television sets
for updates on a
cheating husband's arrival
beautiful skies are sacred
found only on postcards

happy smiles are unusual
only on holidays
never do they stop
to smell the flowers
because there are no flowers

all died
like the dreams and hopes
of single parents' hearts
out in the city
of sleepless nights

walks in the street
to try to find happiness
try to find love in a
city of plastic
what would they give

to touch something real
a real kiss
a real hug
a real friend
a city of silicon smiles

and
ROCK
HARD
HAND
SHAKES

the thought of hope
erased
only time to make money
money is time
time is wasting

because hope is
a hard thing to hold on to
like love and happiness
a hard thing to find
in a fast city of people
made out of
plastic.

War Pigs

In a post war half awakened sleep
dreams consist of mushroom clouds
crying babies and dead bodies
machine gun salutes and maniacs
carrying hearts for souvenirs

amputated children yell for help
while lucky men come out
with both their arms and legs
hunted by agent orange
on foreign lands flags wave for other countries
controlled by coups, world bank loans funding
armies with international conspiracies, hordes
of masked men fighting seven year wars
with no sunlight, clouds of death
covering the villages for weeks, weeping

mothers holding their children
in the palms of their hands
tears hold keys to life and secrets to death
napalm nightmares H-bomb
Hiroshima afternoon massacres
the sky turned the color of dark purple,
the moon casting highlights through the clouds

it looks like death smiling upon us
the absence of hope lingering in the air
the stench of dead cows fouling the lungs of
breath taking survivors on the blackest day
when the sun rose a bloody red made the sky cry
washing away the tears of new dead souls
that await their introduction to eternity

now they walk amongst the living

ghosts with no souls nurtured in the womb of war
born on the day of destruction and desecration
bloody Sunday Sabbath nights
sinful like a politician killing a prostitute
and introducing himself to necrophilia

in a post war dream swarms of locusts
blacken the blue, eclipse the sun, death in the sky,
20 year-olds bleed from their eyes
never had chances to think with their minds
trained to kill without the slightest thought
when the smoke cleared he lay dead and
in the reflection of his eyes, a mushroom cloud

War Pigs
rolling on the floor turning the sky red
War Pigs
annihilators of peace with their blank stares of death
War Pigs
gods of the H-bomb snakes in the grass
War Pigs
the playa giron gang invisible men of glass
War Pigs
the Vieques bombers the Vietcong killers
War Pigs
with their instruments of death
on the heels of humanity
War Pigs
sons of hypocrisy and daughters of conformity
War Pigs
children of colonialism and students of imperialism
War Pigs
makers of holocausts makers of holocausts
War Pigs kill!
War Pigs kill!
War Pigs...kill.

God watches the sweet

Hoping you slept well
looking so innocent
lying there in bed

I only wanted to climb back in
and hold onto your dream
until all the darkness ended
the beautiful night passing with you

listening, watching,
washing, expressing desire
for all the little things
the night offers

comfortable enough to walk around nude
and not feel naked
delicious enough that I try to taste
passion from your skin

the nights bloom to amazing mornings
solar flares desire to try to keep
you satisfied in all this

love has found words made into songs
the experience of intoxicating noises
that make the universe seem complete

the breeze takes invitations from angels
to feed souls, malnourished on a desert
of their own making
trying to fill the holes with fake love and bad sex

tormented by the sight of a crowded room
where you stand in the middle

you're trying to find my eyes and
I'm waiting for you outside

speak to love to be experience
its song
your actions have been epigrams
tattooed on your back

the ink feeds a hollow soul
tormented by moments of anguish
of empty corridors

You still search for me on a street corner
a desert dwelling in your arms
huddled under moonlight
absence of mirage
quenched only by watering eyes filled with life

watch as the sun rises over
Sahara's child held breasted to my chest
imagination drowned in the moon's only tears
the rain's only obsession

I hold onto your dreams
your eyes cast reflections
of a reality with vivid pictures
of nights in your arms

the sun casts shadows on human hearts
the moon rests in the sunsets
the shoulders of god touch her dreams

in limbo souls juxtapose
a statue's pose
to the watchful eyes above

the sweet
your soul is a reflection of god
the moon is a reflection of desire
I hold onto your dreams.

1791 grand concourse: a retrospective

Looking at life through the lens
inherited from the blind
I shall inherit the incompetent senses
of my father and the anger
and impatience of my mother

his nose   her eyes
his lips   her laughter
his ears her compassion
his skin her sense of adventure
their hair

born on the 8th of October
living on the grand concourse
a one bedroom, sunken livingroom
and one sister

a half plywood-half sheetrock wall
made by mother never father
a mother of dark beauty
who had full time jobs being mother,
playing father and supporting us with
bare hands and strong back

nights I watched my sister
and idolized her, realized she is the one
I wanted to grow up to be
no male figures
only uncles
patient or drunk
and a grandfather in the oranges

closet doors were my first canvas
sunken livingroom stomping grounds

all I needed in life was my mother,
my sister and my comics

Then he arrived one day in a Yankee hat
       a beat up old '79 Chevette
       and invited himself into the arms
       of my mother

And I felt I became #2
       he introduced himself to me, his title: Father
       and I didn't understand his language of orders
       I couldn't take it being half the man that I was
       and being told what to do
       from another half a man

When I had a father in a woman
       and another mother in my sister
       I knew how to tie my laces
       throw a baseball, read, write
       and even understand

Why he wasn't there when I was younger
       and why he wanted to be with
       someone else besides my mother

Yet he persisted in squeezing 15 years
       into a matter of months and I got angry
       like any 15 year-old who doesn't want to hear
       anything from his loser father

In the years ahead I saw a lot of him
       sometimes we talked sports
       other times I slammed the door in his face
       reminding people of the women who raised me
       and looking like the man who didn't
       beautiful women as stubborn

as they are strong

I'm the same way and when they say,
        "Oh, you're Katina's brother,"
        I know that will be my epitaph

forever immortalized in my words
        my mother, sister and father
        their existence intertwined in my soul

But to me we'll always be
        Fela, T-Love, Lefty and Bonafide.

She

Razors in her hair
She cuts through all the bullshit
And wants me to love

Vieques

We want to hold you in the morning
for the handful of beauty
that you are, We are grateful

We want to breathe you
in the springtime of your existence
We want to fight in your name
put band aids on your bruises
a crutch under your shoulder

We want to kiss away your worries
so that in the evening when you sleep
you will awake with every limb intact
and whole as it once was

We want people to know your body is not
a wasteland sterilized under the sun
that you're a beautiful woman even with the scars
that you're held me in your breast with for years
and all they do is bite the hand that fed us

Earthquake their ideals that
don't include your well being
a garden's genocide
watch the falling bombs
as they play god and
build cities that scrape skies

Capitalisms hand over cock game
maggie's farm and McDonald's
feed young mouths a processed future
easy on the go, a fast food nation
a community suffocating
under an electrified sky

crackling asthma in
our brother's breath
lungs collapsed colonization

We want to hold you in the afternoon
for the handful of struggle that
you have been since the beginning
We want to breathe you in
the summer of your revolt
against multinational corporations
that make commercials and
donate money to charities to free
themselves from guilt

We want to fight in your name
even if I'm not worthy enough
to understand that this is not a game
this is not something for
a generation to latch on to
to feel like they have done something in life

We want to kiss away your title
of navy playground military base
cops and robbers in backyards
where children play
the South Bronx calls your name
with weak breaths in hunts points
garbage dumps, renovated parks
and play pens, fountain springs bottled water
lead in our cups, asbestos in our walls

Chicago calls your name
while they duck bullets in
the shadow of Humboldt and Logan
metal flags can't protect them

Vieques

We call your name, call for your embrace
60 years your body deteriorates
with every game, set and match

Vieques

Cry your heart
so the world can hear you
your babies are born with cancer
your elders die with cancer

Watch the falling bombs
as your body cries at night
raped by American soldiers
who think they own you
bombs dropping replace roosters' morning calls
empty tanks floating souvenir
missiles lay dormant on your shoulders

Watch the bombs fall like rocks in the water
exploding cancer on the brain
acid in the rain

Vieques

Can you see the tears that bleed from your hands?
can you see the agony in your bones?

The beauty that has been taken away

We want to hold you in the morning
and show you the handful of beauty that you are

Can you see your reflection?

Naturals and Afros

in through the back door
morning expeditions of brothers
and thieves carrying burdens in a bag
insomnia's redeye walks home
entrepreneurs sell their souls
no batteries included

concourse walks in the sunshine
Puerto Rico walks in the rain

A Bronx Tale in b Minor

Mourning After
Lament for Kurt Cobain

Your heart shaped box
is one I've peeked into more than once
your agony rips through skin and bones
striking chords with angst teens
with your four chord songs
about girls and a love buzz

scentless apprentice
of Sabbath, Puppets and Beatles
your sound barrage of
disturbingly lovely frustration

you negative creep walking aneurysm
sunbeam shining anemic royalty
singing over acoustic security
tortured self fulfilling prophecy
on a plain I once walked with
your complaints in my pockets
bottle rockets of your rage explode in recess

they thought you were dumb
maybe you were just trying to be happy
a bleach hair media darling
mainstream addicted to your life
on magazine covers for the world to watch

at 15, I would watch you in programming
circles MTV put in front of me
blooming in your bent notes of hey's and wait's
sing me your songs of depression
never mind, all the pretty packaging
of shiny jewel cases and
angels with exposed stomachs

never mind the stage lights
and screaming fans
just you and your guitar
just play

there was something in the way
you howled with hair over your eyes closed
dreaming the whole world could hear your cries

but they thought it was an act
they saw you in your grunge is dead T-shirt
in pajamas on stage yelling you're not the
only one drowning in a lake of fire
screaming your apologies

your heart shaped box is one I've peeked
into more than once bloomed in riffs and raping
mulattos, albinos, mosquitoes, and libidos

you were the first one I mourned
not Hendrix, not Lennon, not Pac, Not Biggie

you were tears on April 4th
you were pennyroyal tea
you were man who sold the world
you were serving the servants
and on the morning after
I played your music over and over
in remembrance

over windowsills I threw you
an umbilical noose that you never grabbed onto
threw you a lifeline to latch on to
from the media frenzy
the heroine, the permanent circus
the conservatory and the shotgun

how low is low, Kurt?

Your melody is still here
for my older ears to hear
to listen to my childhood in your utero
your songs are still here
in my place for your recovery

your lithium lasted for many years
until bands ripped you off their album covers
and sewed you on their sleeves as inspiration

they pay you respect with overblown
lyrics of egoism and watered down versions
of millionaire angst

Kurt, you swore that you didn't have a gun
did you hum teen spirit in your head

With the lights out it's less dangerous
Here we are now, entertain us

Was that your epitaph,
did you get tired of entertaining us?
Why not another road?
Recluse, exile
change your name quit

but the shotgun is still blasting holes
in Polly's feathers and she still wants water
and your complaints have gone unheard
and your diaries are being read
but your songs will never die
and for that, Kurt
I am forever in debt to your priceless advice

Television
for Angelo "DAGE" Baque

In the television of life
channel eleven shows
visions of hell
fantasies of heaven
and a twilight story zone

the zenith remote control slave
oblivious stares at cable stations
brainwashed soaps
phantom of the opera
in mental operating rooms
with witch doctors
dropping computerized
seduction chips

the $5.95 televised sodomy special
channel 9 UPN, ABC,
Warner Brothers burn
brain cells to a crisp

the mechanical mangler of the mind
home shopping while waiting for the
8 o'clock drive-by
the violence vanguard in
Technicolor tech-9's
home box office explosions

the pay per view
select enter supporter
of the boob tube
that makes you drool
for conspiracies
insert your soul into

the VCR trying to fulfill
your fantasy

dancing with devils
in the pale moonlight
here television blurs
like the poltergeists
with their war of the worlds
costumes on
ready to snatch bodies
at the dawn of the dead

star trekkies lost in space
24 hour marathons supply
fanatics with the thought
of holding onto their
only piece of sanity

the Viacom video slave driver
watching channel zero
every day all day
screens that are concave
new cannibalistic shows
preview on Friday's
reruns repressed wavelengths

amputated mind sets
cut off from all reality
in the land of television
time warns us of
the mighty giants of metropolis rule
with an iron fist in Sony squares
showing world domination specials
for the whole family to watch

CNN stations sucking the sanity

from you, plugging their productions
of imperialism and telling you
what you see is what you get

foxes being chased by peacock eyes
while the family sits by the TV set
to learn a new way to live
in the end TV sets are home teachers and
baby sitters, call it B.O.B.B.
Better Obey Big Brother
named in the mission
of televised genocide

the elite ejaculate on themselves when ratings rise
and when they tell you wrestling and X-files is a fake
you go into a state of shock, you protest the truth
and cry because people die on TV
(as if they're related to your extended family)

they are
playboys on primetime
walking on thin lines
Monday night football fans
dispensing feces on themselves
because they don't want to miss any play action
propaganda being displayed
hail Mary for 2 million dollar commercial spots
they love happy endings
because they are more profitable
think they can fly because
a little boy named peter can
and land themselves in the arms of Mr. Right
stuck behind fiberglass and wood buck

amazing how a story sounds
when it's not giving off subliminal messages

by a plastic family
on a one-hour show
turn off your TV set
naw, not yet
turn it off
MTV is your only god.

Days like this

the sun rises
the alarm rings
stay in bed
the whole world is cold
at 7 in the morning
brush your teeth
wash your face
get dressed
take the world on
watch the traffic
scream at the trains
curse at the buses
catch a morning tag
run from police officers
get on the wrong train
act normal after running
into the wrong train
get back on the right train
get to work late
explain why
make up story
about mother hospitalized
get back to work
restrain self from strangling co-workers
flirt with customers
sell your soul
go on lunch break
eat a pizza
drink a sprite
feel like going home
hobo asking for change
you ask hobo for change
return to work
continue flirting

when manager approaches
look depressed about mother's condition
wink at female employee
act like it didn't hurt
when she acted like she was vomiting
meet millionaire rock star
so high doesn't know who he is
help young hip hop kid
experience Jimi Hendrix for the first time
help young rock kid
experience Public Enemy
for the first time
introduce them to each other
learn they both love Rage against the Machine
meeting of the minds
manager approaches
look depressed
clock out
celebrate life
middle finger your job
watch the business woman notice you staring
curse at the buses
scream at the trains
fight for a seat
read a poem
look at the people on the train
laugh at how weird they are
and they'll laugh at how weird you are
accidentally fall asleep
miss your stop
swear at yourself for falling asleep
see people you used to hang with
but now you think they think they're too cool
to hang with you but they think the same thing about
you
get home

duck bullets
outrun ravenous dogs
hide from police officer
who caught you writing on the wall
make excuses to a friend
who you owe money to
hang on your block
try to explain poetry
to a flock of intoxicated young individuals
they shake their heads
they tell you they used to write poetry
but they're into hanging out now
go upstairs
check your mail
buy your soul back
greet the house
check messages
wrong numbers only
cook pasta
eat food
love your mother
make phone calls
stare at your books
realize you haven't read half of them
look at Jimi
play your guitar
the moon has risen once again
the wind whispers your name
the bed calls for you to rest your body
to recuperate your soul
rebuild your stamina for the next day
and know that you are blessed for
surviving a day like this.

Rojas

He's a myth on our tongue
a story told around rum and cokes
grandfather was a gambling man
who when father was born inherited his name,
his hands, his roll of the dice, his flip of the card,
red was his favorite color,
red reverberates in our family history,
red is the color of our name

Rojas.

in New York City, father carries his name,
a left handed fast talker, and infidel like his father
a knife carrying punk because the South Bronx
isn't a place where you think
you're the man without showing it,
years in places for stabbing souls leaking from wounds,
Hicksville, Otisville, Comstock, Riker's
hold his adolescence and early adulthood
in the cracks of the granite and rust of the bars
the shadows hold his tears while sleeping

Rojas.

1971, fatherhood to baby girl tattooed
on his chest, Katina smiles wide across
lead paint walls, St. Jerome's church plays backdrop
in a neighborhood where salsa ran in the streets
and bomba played in the casitas
of old jibaros holding onto tradition.
streets where father ran with cousins who were shady
in character, unfaithful in trust but father lived,
lived through stabbings and years of cold echoes
bouncing off his ears in solitude

Rojas.

in 1977, I was born with smiles wide across
walls in a concourse household, left-handed
fast talker no longer lingering, ruby colored heartbeats,
burgundy breaths, a mother's celebration of our
crimson existence, I inherited grandfather's roll
of the dice, his nervous twitch when the smell
of oxygen is paired with blackjack,
inherited father's infidelities and insecurities

I inherited his face, his smile, his skin
but I am my mother's son, hyphenate my name
like she did, Nazario-Rojas, follow sister's footsteps
Rojas-Nazario, create another identity

let the R in Rojas stand for ravage, rapture, ravishing,
rebellion, rejoiced, requiem, responsibility, revolution,
risky, rhetoric, rhapsody, romantic, rose

Rojas will never be a beautiful rose
blooming a burgundy celebration of a family's line
a scarlet shine over our accomplishments
our name will never be beautiful

Rojas.
will always be our blood bleeding
Rojas.
will always be my tears falling
Rojas.
will always be my mother crying
Rojas.
will always be my sister yelling
Rojas.
will always be my father apologizing

but I am changing it, father
I am changing to make our name as gorgeous
as a red mural on a white wall
a magenta colorizing our life line
from a decade old gray
transforming decades of despair
with our blood flowing
decades of disappointment,
with our bonds growing
years of grief without our tradition written
a metamorphosis from a tragedy to a triumph

I am changing it, father
to make our name as brilliant as beautiful
as the color red, one day our name
will be a beautiful red.

Paper Maiche Heart

the paper maiche heart
I made for her was only for a day
a cold day with gray on its face
slush on its feet
flurries from its eyes falling
flowers nailed upside down on
walls of fury and hate
patience and love

Ever dream in the summer moonlight?
loser, she called me
because I made her unhappy
she didn't want to be with me
because I walked on a thin fantastic line
and never knew what I wanted in life
said I was trapped in my make believe world
of guitars and poetry in a room with
three and a half walls and four windows
with adolescent posters of my heroes

she was a strange woman
that's probably why I liked her so much
she was spontaneous and wild
yet responsible
lectured me when I had no money
and always left her wallet at home
so she wouldn't spend any of her money

I told her that I loved her one day
uh huh was her response and I knew what she meant
she was looking for conviction in my voice
she said that I sounded like an idiot

I tried telling her how I feel
and she would say that I feel like an idiot
so after that I never talked about love

because to her I was an idiot
who was in love with her and she loved
every minute of it
she would whisper I like you
to make it seem like she was saying I love you

then say she was just playing,
she would tell me she likes having me around
because I made her laugh and that I was good in bed
as long as I wasn't mechanical
and made it exciting or interesting
but I wanted more than a woman
I can make funny faces at and perform fellatio for

I wanted a woman to introduce
me to new ideals and new things
someone stimulating, not just there

then I saw her
she was on the D train going downtown
a red skirt with a white top
nice toes, long curly hair
and succulent lips
red like blood
reading Neruda's "Canto General"

I read her name from her skin
she sat across from me, smiled
I was a shivering buffoon
I knew it, she knew it, everyone on the train knew it
I was sweating and my once dry orange seat
was soaking wet

she giggled but I had no courage to talk to her
I sat there dumbfounded and staring
with a huge grin on my face
and finally gathered enough cojones
to talk to her as the train
pulled into Broadway-Lafayette
and then she disappeared
into a crowded station
and I sat there with my failure
in my lap

one day I'll see her again and
when I do I'll have a
paper maiche heart for her.

Iron Wheels

the propaganda machine
started with
keys of oppression
screams in the fields of
nuclear death games

no hesitation to pull the lever
flick the switch burning glory
American supremacy rallies

the aimless run like
headless donkeys and
anorexic elephants
democracy & truth
wrapped by the noose of
uncle Sam's deception
police display their
silver badge swastikas

brutalized by the sons of
the four fathers
harassed by the pigs of patriarchy
desensitized by television sets of
subliminal senator's suicide on primetime

the agenda of justice is adjourned
the 1st amendment is a wooden
paddle spanked on the butts of
the advocates of American society

in a land where dreams of freedom
cease and skylines burn
tyranny waves over buildings

Bonafide Rojas

casting images of racism raping liberty
in the backyard of freedom

monopolies hang the lower class
with dollar made nooses
squeezing hope from
the pores of their carcasses

monkeys in the senate
parlor tricks and hoops
marching down Broadway
the parade walking on people's backs
with their feet synchronized
the marching band
holding rifles and shotguns
instruments of destruction
beating people into submission

their music of madness
on a rampaging crusade
playing death hymns
in memory of revolutionaries
they never acknowledged
but played them because they liked
the morbid sound of it all

the empire takes shots to their backs
as target practice makes perfect
walking over the face of humanity
hypocrisy's laughter echoes

institutionalized into super structures
and super information highways
fed aggression and conformity
taught brutality tactics
deals with devils and angels

bulls in blue
running and parading
stampeding life

the propaganda machine of
America's dream is rolling
unseen, confused and dazed

the band on a rampage
branded barcodes on
the minds of zombie wall street
stock markets crashing
maritime law cohorts

assimilated ignorance
crowds of concentrated
campers of major corporations
plans of NAFTA
masters of third world sweatshops
chopping off body parts of children of labor

worlds apart from the dream of freedom
America's strangle and mangle
holding the earth by a noose
the writing on walls
yelling for help

the American inquisition
vice grip holds people's brains
selling themselves to plastic gods
high ranking stars and world police stripes
IMF and world bank plans
stars five pointed pentagrams
scorching suns on the bodies
of chained factory workers

with their dreams on chokehold
until they're off the clock

the big band of imperialism
hammering sickles
in the heads of communists
captured and beheaded
by the conglomerate

death walks with the red, white and blue
and top-hat of uncle Sam
saying he wants you

and at the crack of dawn
the big band played
death hymns for people they
never acknowledged
but played them anyway
because they like
the morbid sound of it all.

Feels like forever

In the morning when the sun rose, her face
absorbed all the light and lit my life
spotlighted in the midnight's breath of love
twelve hours are never enough to enjoy
every inch of her, while the start of my days
always falling short of forever

She once asked me, "How long is forever"
and a question mark appeared on my face
"Well, forever is as long as my days
and until the end of my life"
"Would that be enough time to enjoy
us," she asked me.
"How long is your love"

Well, long was the wrong word.
"How deep is your love"
should be the question. "Is your love forever"
and I thought about the nights we enjoy
and the nights we despise with the blank stare
on my face still lingering.
My love is longer than my life
which is longer than all of my days

Which makes it as close to forever as possible.
Our days
carried on and we carried on our acts of love
through every cycle of our lives
together and some of those days went on forever
and through those long hours of writing, my face
hasn't always had enjoy

all the hours we shared, I did love and enjoy
her in all her beauty and what she offered my days
and we always tried to put smiles
on each other's faces.
Every inch of my body was put here to love
her every fabric of being, forever
One song we hated was "You light up my life"

But Stevie Wonder's "Songs in the key of Life"
was our soundtrack. As much as we did enjoy
Stevie, Nina Simone's Wild is the Wind will forever
stand the test of time as her favorite song. For days
she would cry to that song and just
to get it out of her system.
I love Hendrix and she could tell
by the look on my face

she mimics my face knowing Jimi is life to me
and I love the fact that she knows that and the way
we enjoy our days
feels like they should last
forever.

A Bronx tale in b minor

two:13 p.m.
the D train station at 125th Street
waiting for   the orange circle
                      underground silver horse

uptown bound boogie down
landscapes of ambulance sirens
the trash at 161st stadium sunsets
            crack spots to rock
            empty clips in the sky
            nine raised high
            ten seconds to live

area codes tell the black top smell
in the air only a few live to tell stories of hell
cops on killing rages, death's a black sunday
twelve year-olds pose their lives away
picture framed

D train arrives roaring
orange seats, poles, bums and a hole in my jeans
searing guitar screams, air guitar swings
dreams on the heads of wishful emcees
and minority Puerto Rican punks
lost in swirls of hip hop influence
dreaming in salsa twists
rock and roll blasts of wanting to be different
pushing their ethnic breakdowns
farther than their parents ever pushed it to,
hip hop claimed their youth
the Bronx claimed their home

Fordham Road summer daze,
mini skirts halter topped

orchard 12 the last stop
fire hydrants blasting on
hanging outside until dawn
playing capicu in front of the bodega

basketball is a gated playground
greco-roman coliseum full courts
football in the streets
milk crates the spectators' seats
they watch in amazement
kennedy pizza dollar treats
death defying escape acrobatics
radios blasting the lasted heat wave

five periods of life
depressed because you go to schools
shadowed in the presence
of old american presidents
disconnected from neighborhoods

in through the back door
morning expeditions of brothers
and thieves carrying burdens in a bag
insomnia's redeye walks home
entrepreneurs sell their souls
no batteries included

concourse walks in the sunshine
Puerto Rico walks in the rain

hung juries and crooked cops
tourist visits historic hip hop sites
guided by gentrified hands
to lead the offensive of the low property
real estate game, the jewel of a landowner's
family name

where people's faces
linger in the wind of poverty

and when the Yankee games are over
they run back to their lower Manhattan duplexes,
New Rochelle mansions, New Jersey ranches
and talk of the inhabitants
of The Concourse and Webster,
Jerome and Tremont,
West Farms and Parkchester,
Co-op City and University,
Mott Haven and Hunts Point.

talk of our existence
our savagery, our cannibalism
our strength to live in rat infested
roach ingested asbestos schools
precincts lockdown projects
schoolyards are playgrounds
spoffard cellblock screams
elevated 4, 5, 6 dreams
seven one eight, 10453
the boogie down Bronx
talking of our existence.

The Red Muse

1. 6 Hours Apart

over the orange skyline
I start to stare at the sun
clouds form figments from
my imagination
surreal images of you

your night is almost
halfway through its slumber
your breaths turn to circles
of devotion, a maze of dreams
trying to fall off the cliff into reality

the phone rings at 12 o'clock
your voice vibrates into my dream
your mornings are escapades into
my midnight blues and purples
highlighted moons glowing

full through my room to
serenade my sleep with
a beautiful woman who
slipped into my existence
fell into my world

a shooting star and
like a Shakespearean play
at the dawn of midnight
the dusk of morning dances
in sun rays

words jumping off my tongue
tattooed on my arms for

remembrance and escape
her breaths feel right
when the sun rises over my head

the nights are beautiful enough
to impressively compare you with
and through all of this
you're still not in front of me
but I wait 6 hours apart
blue from the start even
red through the beginnings
rightly bright the yellow burst
orange blast
the dull life nova's flame

light the sky
incredible burgundy highlights
colors around the rim of my vision
the canvas I paint every night
but smoothly with my hand

never overworked but should
I just gaze at the existence
that is you
I'll compare you and I see differences
in all your alter egos and

closely I'll add color and life
to each of you
then you alone are my favorite
for today is the first day
I've really lived

I've seen the world through
an unbiased eye
I know what it is to be loved

under the pale moonlight
writing love sonnets

an affection never known
to be my own
a warm feeling succumbing
and I know one day
you'll return to my arms

never known to you
yet they'll feel just right
because they belong to you
6 hours apart
one day you'll return

2. The Sleepless Night

In these days of wandering confusion
the poems I've written about
you give me solace
they put me in a world all my own

you give me sanity in times
I'm going to crack
then I think about your position
how you showed me how strong you are
and I find the strength to go on

Everyday I walked in a sea of unknown faces
wondering if you're walking past me

teasing me
the wind whispering
your name to me

And I'm found staring aimlessly
into eyes mirrored in strange reflections
and sweet serenading voices
that feed my soul in a time of

Lone   li   ness

You are the guiding light in
these days of wonder
the sun is setting around 6 o'clock
which means I will be
on the corner of
oblivion and nowhere
yelling your name at the sun

answering me in flickers of fire
and eclipses of the moon

I sleep late at night
staring at the phone
asking it to ring
picking it up
making sure there is a dial tone

Counting the minutes
as they turn to hours
hours as they turn to days
clouds to rain
winds to cyclones
a million nights turn to a million days

I sit

in a dark living room with
my guitar on my lap
playing songs to vibrate

off the window back to me

I've been called crazy
In this time of relationship
I cherish your conversations

more than breaths
more than deaths
more than life
more than births

I cannot exist without you

the
        anticipa
                        tion
is killing me

but I try to cope with the
stabbing feelings
on my back while I sleep

for a minute there
I lose myself in my sleep
In dreams of landscapes
I created for you because
You   can't   be   here

I'm left with a reminder of
your essence in phone calls
I've memorized and written
down on my forearms
paragraph breaks and all

Your signature at the end
of each bone cartilage

each letter of your name
etched on my knuckles

7 pieces of my soul
connected with ink on skin
a ring
that sits on my finger
waiting for you
never has known you
never has felt your
hairs prickle against the metal

a Hebrew sentence
tells me how to feel
how to become obsessed
and immersed
but all I can do is wait

sitting at the edge of my bed
at the middle of night
with my guitar on my lap
waiting patiently for your return

or your first arrival
in the arms of my existence

3. *Blind Man's Muse*

darkness
the noon time sun
everyday I pray to see
the sunrise
everyday I hear her voice
linger in my head
holding conversations

with echoes

I stare
at white walls
see confusion in the cracks
paradoxes of love

waiting patiently besides
my shadow's side
for her second arrival

her first introduction
was her voice
playing with me as if
I was a blind man
thinking that her
voice is all I needed
to put me through hard times

her voice entranced
the inner workings
of my head to build
shrines of sound for her
so when I need to hear her voice
I shatter a shrine each time to
reverberate in my head
for days to satisfy the thirst I had

she once asked me
"Would you write poems
about me when we're eighty"
and I felt her wanting to be
with me forever

me

a silly poet
love struck with a voice
and walking without sight
and she wanted to know
my answer

"Of course I would"

she would speak into me
to identify herself
she would describe
scents of her hair
strawberries and peaches

I can hear her breaths
fluttering butterflies
born in the womb
of a caterpillar's whispers

beauty wound in her hair
each one
 tracing her soul
from scalp to foot
I hold in the palms
of my hands
tightly one of her breaths

morning sunrises
each layer colored
one over another
a divine mural made only for us
because the only thing
we can share is the sky

I wait on the other side of the planet
patiently

I close my eyes
when I think
playing the part of
the blind man
trying to feel his way
to her face
to her body

my eyesight is useless
in this position
I will play the blind man
in my dreams of darkness
with lighted silhouettes
with the moon exposing the
curves of her body

I can see her
when I close
my eyes

I can feel her
when I close
my eyes

I can hear her
when I close
my eyes

I can love her
when I close
my eyes

but not forever
I want my sight back

4. *Long Rendezvous*

forever
would I wait?
under the full moon
of our love

in a desert field
of our dreams
I would make an oasis
for our rest

in a crowded street
I sketch an S.O.S.
so you can walk over
to save me

I will write poetry
on trains from New York
to Paris writing
"Prenez ma vole, ma muse"

I will be waiting
with open arms under
a Barcelona sun
or in the madness of Times Square

Patience
with poems on my skin
to offer as a gift
or a password

To our hearts
To show we are the ones
We've been waiting for
Over the past 77 years

Through rain and sleet
Where the sun never meets
My fingertips
Wind and snow

Where my lips touch
The cheeks of tomorrow's
Whisper
that speaks of destiny's path

Open for me
Waiting to walk but I wait
On the pavement of her
Desire talking to the sky

The sky watches us wait
For each other with
hands slide past thighs
on crowded London streets

I will wait at La Defense
at the statue park of erected poles
staring at the
Arc de Triomphe

Waiting for her to come
rescue me from my
long rendezvous but until
then I've promised to wait

I've promised to be patient
Like I have since the beginning
But the sun is starting to
Melt my poems

My tears are stinging my hands
from the etching
of your name
7 scars for 7 letters

the poems on my skin are
deteriorating from the
screams of winter's thunder
smeared words but

never smeared patience
the sun is setting
and my feet haven't
moved in years
imprinted my soul
on concrete's face
all I have is her voice
in my head saying hello

that dream is enough
for me to wait another
77 years with more hope
and more poems

with healed skin and
a healed hand and a new sun
with new hope and new desire
to love like I've never loved before

5. The White Room (Mosaics of Red)

So there she sits
in front of these
tainted glass of eyes

traveling hours across
America

I saw the sun rise
on mountain tops
Watched
as it ran down the sky
and at the mouth of the Atlantic
I bathed in mosaics of red

In my arms
she sits in contemplation
talks of the world
its evils and love

Blue-eyed amazement
torn and scarred
in the eyes of Huracán
fasting under hot suns

I stand in the middle of
highways and area codes
two steps behind her last breath
leaving laments of my past death
two seconds ago

I sit in her presence   Naked
holding the truth of my love in hand
I shed my current life to
start a new one with her

Holding her heart
patchwork puzzles
put together
collages of midnights

Around wrists dangle
red necklaces
I peel the affection
from my tongue
place it on her lips
swallows whole and
she accepts my gift
offering a new way
to look at life

Close her eyes
Open her soul
Close her mouth
Open her heart

The truth in her voice
holds gravity's dance
700 pieces of her soul
ordered to create
a shining

Blind sight
walking affection
I've found the red muse
in the middle of a symphony of music

A reminder of
sun
          moon
stars

rebirth every morning
from the evening's madness
hours blink to rest
her torn body to heal
to whisper in her ear

sonnets guided by moonlight

life in a white room
we stare at each other
while we sleep
I found the universe in her hair
Bliss in her smile
A bare face on the canvas
of my hand
I kiss to resurrect
her image every time

at the mouth of the Atlantic
I yell her name to the sun
while she yells mine to the moon
I swallow inspiration
exhaling devotion
while the symphony
plays in my head
bathing in mosaics of red

6. *Morning XIX*

the next morning
the sun was brighter than ever
it held your face in the light
angelic
swimming in your eyes

the rest of the world is obsolete
time stands still
noosed watches on strangles
to stop ticks from ending
my trip

three days stretched across
infinity for infinity
hands held melted through
skin and bones
one never leaving the other

Siamese
skin to skin
back to back
hands play with hands
naked
apple halves cut
down the split of your back

vines and stars
intertwined in your hair
I whisper in your ear
haikus of your
inspiration

wherever you go
I'll always
follow to love you

declarations on crowded streets
cylinders staircases
spotlighted benchmarks
of our love

mantras repeated
to seep through
speaking into palms
to massage pressure points
vibrations of hands

love me
like
I love you

five times
waiting for the sunrise
five months
waiting to open my eyes

a blind touch becomes
Sight
fingertips are guides
on your body

hills and hills
curves that entrance in
dim moonlight smiling
I take the light
place it in your mouth
swallowed

wild as the wind
passion
holds our bodies tight
in the eye of the moon

serenaded by the breeze
serenaded by the breeze

our bodies grew
to expand over one another
filling parts of my
hollow shell

Your skin and saliva
destined for me

In you, love hides
behind your heart
giggling in the sunrise

thank you for existing
and giving reason
to write on my soul

to express thoughts
through words
divinely given
because I know you'll
always listen with
arms out
and with a soul to share.

Gabriel's Trumpet
for Gabriel Garcia Marquez

> In the end all he will have is a corpse
> and some poems stuffed in his ribcage

Life: (un)titled

I've tried to edit my life into just good verses
of my existence, but life isn't a great poem
So a bad stanza or two will live in the piece

An indentation for my childhood
a run-on sentence for my adolescence
and a semicolon for puberty

Italics on my education
bold type for my first and last love
and underlines for the importance of family

Spanglish and an upside down
exclamation point for heritage
a grammatical error for neighborhood
a coma after 14, 21, and eventually 30,
to keep life going

I'll make the font either Arial Black or Impact
so it can represent my ego, then
Times New Roman size 11 to show growth

I'll break life mid-sentence, 2 breaths per page
an asterisk for a song lyric
representing a period in me

I'll keep it single spaced, so the words don't
outlive the life in length and I'll keep the poem
on the left side of the page,

because I tried to stay on the left side of life
but once in a while a moment or word can stray right
trying to be free verse

No meter in my lines
Rhyming was never a strong point for me
Chicago knows they have jokes for my freestyle sessions

Wingdings to represent my outlandish behavior
a period to show closure for my animosity for my father
a question mark for my career

A haiku to show how I should be in life
An epic on how I tend to be
Simplicity is something I've strived for

There will be five parts to this piece
by the time I expire in breaths and heartbeats
NYC, Chicago with sub-sections, Love, struggle

And the fifth yet to be titled, but it'll be
multilingual to show my pilgrimage back
to Puerto Rico, Latin America and my love for travel

And in the end there will be
            no pseudonym, no moniker
            no Graff tag, no hip hop title
            no acronym
            no performance
            no Puerto Rican with hair who loved
            rock and roll and Che Guevara
            no Bonafide,
            hopefully no regrets, hopefully

It'll be Steven Rojas
born October 8th, 1977
loved his family and took poetry serious enough
to call himself a poet
and have poems represent
his life.

Spanish/English Glossary

Pelo Bueno: Good Hair

Boleros: Ballads

Vieques: one of several islands belonging to the Puerto Rican archipelago.

Uvas: Grapes

Campesinos: Farmers, workers of the soil.

Chiapas: Mountain region in Mexico, home of the Zapatistas

Albizu: Pedro Albizu Campos, Puerto Rican Freedom Fighter and leader of the Nationalist Party.

Giron: Cuban beach Area, site of the 1962 Bay of Pigs Invasion by CIA-sponsored Cuban exiles living in the U.S.

Cienfuegos: Camilo Cienfuegos, Cuban revolutionary hero who fought alongside Fidel Castro and Che Guevara. Died in a plane crash just before the corrupt Bautista regime fell in 1959.

Aqui: Here

Taino: Indigenous people of the Caribbean

Nueva Yol: New York

Griot: Mandingo word for poet, wordsmith, historian.

Yo Soy Negro: I am Black.

Boogaloo: Latino dance music mixing R&B and Cha-cha-cha, circa late-1960s.

Neruda: Pablo Neruda, among the great Chilean poets of the 20th Century.

Jibaros: agricultural workers, homeboys, farmers. In Puerto Rican cosmology, the typical down-to-earth person.

Capicu: When a player ends a Domino game with a double digit on each end of the board or with a double six, thereby demonstrating skill and strategy.

Guayaberas: A Caribbean shirt, pleated and usually with four pockets; considered appropriate dress for all occasions.

Cuando te vas a cortal ese pelo: When are you going to cut that hair?

Nunca: Never

Loisaida: Spanish variation for the Lower East Side, a section of New York City's Manhattan Island.

SAMO: Jean Michel Basquiat's and his Graffiti partner, Al Diaz's Tag. The graffiti tag calls up associations like "Sambo," "Samson," or "Same Old Shit". A Tag identifies the graffiti writer and his credentials like initials.

Suheir: Suheir Hammad, a local New York poet of Palestinian descent.

Madre: Mother

Bomba y Plena: Two Puerto Rican musical forms, both of which are rooted in African influences.

Groupito: Small Group of people

Rojas: Red

Prenez ma vole, ma muse: (French) Would you like to be my Muse?

Dark Souls Enterprises is a Nuyorican owned, multimedia company dedicated to promoting and preserving the visual, oral, and literary traditions of the African Diaspora.

Our Dark Souls Press catalog line includes:

Sancocho
A Book of Nuyorican Poetry

Nuyorican Dreams - Live CD
3rd Annual Voices for the Voiceless

Yemaya Y Ochun - Live CD
4th Annual Voices for the Voiceless

The Freedom Song - Live CD
5th Annual Voices for the Voiceless

Palabras
A Book of Nuyorican Sights and Sounds